# Praise for *The Joy of Discipleship*

*"The capacity for joy takes its root in hope. Pope Francis is our generation's prophet of hope and thus our prophet of joy. This is him at his best, befuddling our unhappy categories, offering a vision of hope and mercy, and showing us in his own person the joy found in an earthy, cheerful discipleship."*

—Ronald Rolheiser OMI, President, Oblate School of Theology

*"According to Pope Francis, God's compassionate love for us and our responsibility to love one another, especially the poor and marginalized, are central to evangelization. God's love fills us with joy, which we want to share with others. Francis preaches the Gospel, not the catechism. He is more concerned about how we live our faith than how we explain it."*

—Thomas J. Reese, SJ, Senior Analyst, *National Catholic Reporter* and author of *Inside the Vatican: The Politics and Organization of the Catholic Church*

*"If one is seeking inspiration from Pope Francis,* The Joy of Discipleship *is the best compilation out there."*

—Mark E. Thibodeaux, SJ, author of *God's Voice Within* and *Reimagining the Ignatian Examen*

"*Pope Francis is a truly happy man. He radiates joy, love, and indescribable peace. All this comes through, too, in this fine collection of his homilies, talks, and writings, compiled and edited by James Campbell. I feel sure that those who read these inspiring pages will be enriched and experience something of that joy, love, and peace expressed through the life of our beloved pope.*"
—Elisabetta Piqué, Correspondent for *La Nación* and author of *Pope Francis: Life and Revolution*

"*James Campbell's seamless compilation brings out the extraordinary vitality of Pope Francis's message of joy and mercy spoken to a wounded world. The gospel is 'good news.' Christ is alive. The Holy Spirit is at work, bringing hope and healing. The pope has something important to say—listen to him!*"
—Jim Manney, author of *A Simple, Life-Changing Prayer* and *What's Your Decision?*

# Praise for *Walking with Jesus*

*"Magnificent. A beautiful invitation by a truly holy man to meet the one at the center of his life: Jesus Christ."*
—James Martin, SJ, author of *Jesus: A Pilgrimage*

*"Pope Francis knows that the encounter with Jesus Christ puts our lives on a new path. Our life of faith is a journey that we are making with Jesus—walking with him, sharing his life, traveling in the company of brothers and sisters who have accepted his invitation: 'Follow me.' In this inspiring book, our Holy Father offers us bread for the journey—to deepen our friendship with Jesus and our fellowship in continuing his mission of mercy in our world."*
—Most Reverend José H. Gomez, Archbishop of Los Angeles

*"A wonderfully inspiring and stirring resource capturing the depth of Pope Francis's magnificent vision and mission. His powerful message speaks of the richness of Catholic story and tradition.* Walking with Jesus: A Way Forward for the Church *is an exceptional source of wisdom and guidance for all involved in the ministry of religious education."*
—Edith Prendergast, RSC, Director of Religious Education, Archdiocese of Los Angeles

*"What a wonderful addition to our knowledge of the fresh and inspiring message of a revolutionary pope from 'the ends of the earth!'"*
—Allan Figueroa Deck, SJ, Casassa Chair and Professor of Theology, Loyola Marymount University

# Praise for *The Church of Mercy* by Pope Francis

*"This collection offers fascinating insight into the mind and heart of someone who has rapidly become one of the world's most beloved public figures."*
—Publishers Weekly

*"Refreshingly humane, focusing on people rather than institutions. Admirers of Francis and students of Church history alike will find this a useful introduction to the pontiff's thought."*
—Kirkus Reviews

*"A refreshing book, a true treasure chest of wisdom, which will both comfort and unsettle any attentive reader."*
—Englewood Review of Books

*"I can't even tell you the sense of wonder and gratitude I am feeling reading* The Church of Mercy. *Every Christian in at least the western world should read this man . . . at least read enough to know what Christianity has come upon or been given or will be watching develop over the next few years. This man sees, and is of, the Kingdom of God."*
—Phyllis Tickle, author of *The Great Emergence*

# *The*
# JOY
## *of*
# DISCIPLESHIP

# *The* JOY *of* DISCIPLESHIP

## Reflections from Pope Francis on Walking with Christ

BY

# POPE FRANCIS

Edited and compiled by
James P. Campbell

LOYOLAPRESS.
A JESUIT MINISTRY
Chicago

## LOYOLA PRESS.
### A JESUIT MINISTRY

3441 N. Ashland Avenue
Chicago, Illinois 60657
(800) 621-1008
www.loyolapress.com

Cover art credit: Franco Origlia/GettyImages

**Hardcover**

ISBN-13: 978-0-8294-4387-5
ISBN-10: 0-8294-4387-8

**Paperback**

ISBN-13: 978-0-8294-4431-5
ISBN-10: 0-8294-4431-9
Library of Congress Control Number: 2015955630

Printed in the United States of America.
16 17 18 19 20 21 22 Bang 10 9 8 7 6 5 4 3 2 1

# CONTENTS

# Foreword

One word that has most often summarized the teaching ministry of Pope Francis is *mercy*, the mercy of God toward us and the response to that mercy that we, his people, must also manifest. No less important a word for the pope is *joy*. When the love of God, poured out in mercy, touches us, it cannot help but produce joy and gladness. The Holy Father has repeatedly spoken of the human heart's desire for joy. The joy of the disciple is a deeper reality, a joy that comes from the closeness of God, the closeness of God in our lives. "Surprised" by this joy, we are compelled to witness to it. This witnessing is the mark of a true disciple of Jesus Christ.

James P. Campbell has gathered together sections of Pope Francis's homilies, speeches, and other documents and orchestrated them into several themes that specify the reality of Christian joy. The book is a kind of modern-day catena, or chain, each citation a link that highlights a facet of the joy of a disciple. One facet is Christ's resurrection, another is the presence of God in the family, another is the Church, and still another is the Holy Spirit as the soul of mission and of joy. In all, some eleven topics are considered with one goal in mind: to describe how the realities expressed by the pope on each topic bring about, enhance, or challenge us as disciples of JOY. For Pope Francis, joy is contagious and becomes a verification principle for a beloved son or daughter as a witness to Jesus Christ.

The Holy Father has spoken or written, even in his brief time as pope, on almost every dimension of discipleship. Campbell's selections admirably pull together such a wide array of topics on the pope's mind and the relevance of the life of Jesus to our joy, even the "hidden life" of Christ when there went by those seemingly endless days of quiet unobtrusive activity on his part. Pope Francis has advised us to "read the Gospel, carry a little Gospel with us." Campbell has created a mosaic of the pope's words on Gospel joy. This volume also gives us a portrait of the pope himself, and what amazing joy fills his life, his mind, his teaching—in short, his discipleship!

Daniel Cardinal DiNardo
Archbishop of Galveston-Houston

# 1

# The Extraordinary Year of Mercy

*Excerpts from Pope Francis's Papal Bull of April 11, 2015*

*Francis, Bishop of Rome, servant of the servants of God,*

*To all who read this letter: Grace, Mercy, and Peace*

1. Jesus Christ is the face of the Father's mercy. These words might well sum up the mystery of the Christian faith. Mercy has become living and visible in Jesus of Nazareth, reaching its culmination in him. The Father, "rich in mercy" (Ephesians 2:4), after having revealed his name to Moses as "a God merciful and gracious, slow to anger, and abounding in steadfast love and faithfulness" (Exodus 34:6), has never ceased to show, in various ways throughout history, his divine nature. In the "fullness of time" (Galatians 4:4), when everything had been arranged according to his plan of salvation, he sent his only Son into the world, born of the Virgin Mary, to reveal his love for us in a definitive way. Whoever sees Jesus sees the Father (see John 14:9). Jesus of Nazareth, by his words, his actions, and his entire person reveals the mercy of God.

7. "For his mercy endures forever." This is the refrain that repeats after each verse in Psalm 136 as it narrates the history of God's revelation. By virtue of mercy, all the events of the Old Testament are replete with profound salvific import. Mercy renders God's history with Israel a history of salvation. To repeat continually "for his mercy endures forever," as the psalm does, seems to break through the dimensions of space and time, inserting everything into the eternal mystery of love. It is as if to say that not only in history, but for

all eternity man will always be under the merciful gaze of the Father. It is no accident that the people of Israel wanted to include this psalm—the "Great *Hallel*," as it is called—in its most important liturgical feast days.

Before his Passion, Jesus prayed with this psalm of mercy [Psalm 136]. Matthew attests to this in his Gospel when he says that "when they had sung a hymn" (Matthew 26:30), Jesus and his disciples went out to the Mount of Olives. While he was instituting the Eucharist as an everlasting memorial of himself and his paschal sacrifice, he symbolically placed this supreme act of revelation in the light of his mercy. Within the very same context of mercy, Jesus entered upon his passion and death, conscious of the great mystery of love that he would consummate on the Cross. Knowing that Jesus himself prayed this psalm makes it even more important for us as Christians, challenging us to take up the refrain in our daily lives by praying these words of praise: "for his mercy endures forever."

8. With our eyes fixed on Jesus and his merciful gaze, we experience the love of the Most Holy Trinity. The mission Jesus received from the Father was that of revealing the mystery of divine love in its fullness. "God is love" (1 John 4:8:16), John affirms for the first and only time in all of Holy Scripture. This love has now been made visible and tangible in Jesus' entire life. His person is nothing but love, a love given gratuitously. The relationships he forms with the people who approach him manifest something entirely unique and unrepeatable. The signs he works, especially in favor of sinners, the poor, the marginalized, the sick, and the suffering, are all meant to teach mercy. Everything in him speaks of mercy. Nothing in him is devoid of compassion.

9. . . . Jesus affirms that mercy is not only an action of the Father, but it also becomes a criterion for ascertaining who his true children are. In short, we are called to show mercy because mercy has first been shown to us. Pardoning offenses becomes the clearest expression of merciful love, and for us Christians it is an imperative from which we cannot excuse ourselves. At times how hard it seems to forgive! And yet pardon is the instrument placed into our fragile hands to attain serenity of heart. To let go

> *Jesus affirms that mercy is not only an action of the Father, but it also becomes a criterion for ascertaining who his true children are.*

of anger, wrath, violence, and revenge are necessary conditions to living joy-fully. Let us therefore heed the Apostle's exhortation: "Do not let the sun go down on your anger" (Ephesians 4:26). Above all, let us listen to the words of Jesus, who made mercy an ideal of life and a criterion for the credibility of our faith: "Blessed are the merciful, for they shall obtain mercy" (Matthew 5:7) is the beatitude to which we should particularly aspire in this Holy Year.

10. Mercy is the very foundation of the Church's life. All of her pastoral activity should be caught up in the tenderness she makes present to believers; nothing in her preaching and in her witness to the world can be lacking in mercy. The Church's very credibility is seen in how she shows merciful and compassionate love. The Church "has an endless desire to show mercy." . . . The time has come for the Church to take up the joyful call to mercy once more. It is time to return to the basics and to bear the weaknesses and strug-gles of our brothers and sisters. Mercy is the force that reawakens us to new life and instills in us the courage to look to the future with hope.

12. The Church's first truth is the love of Christ. The Church makes herself a servant of this love and mediates it to all people: a love that forgives and expresses itself in the gift of oneself. Consequently, wherever the Church is present, the mercy of the Father must be evident. In our parishes, commu-nities, associations, and movements—in a word, wherever there are Chris-tians—everyone should find an oasis of mercy.

14. The Lord Jesus shows us the steps of the pilgrimage to attain our goal: "Judge not, and you will not be judged; condemn not, and you will not be condemned; forgive, and you will be forgiven; give, and it will be given to you; good measure, pressed down, shaken together, running over, will be put into your lap. For the measure you give will be the measure you get back" (Luke 6:37–38). The Lord asks us above all *not to judge* and *not to condemn.* If anyone wishes to avoid God's judgment, he should not make himself the judge of his brother or sister.

15. It is my burning desire that . . . the Christian people may reflect on the *corporal and spiritual works of mercy.* It will be a way to reawaken our con-science, too often grown dull in the face of poverty. And let us enter more

deeply into the heart of the Gospel where the poor have a special experience of God's mercy. Jesus introduces us to these works of mercy in his preaching so that we can know whether or not we are living as his disciples. Let us rediscover these *corporal works of mercy*: to feed the hungry, give drink to the thirsty, clothe the naked, welcome the stranger, heal the sick, visit the imprisoned, and bury the dead. And let us not forget the *spiritual works of mercy:* to counsel the doubtful, instruct the ignorant, admonish sinners, comfort the afflicted, forgive offenses, bear patiently those who do us ill, and pray for the living and the dead.

We cannot escape the Lord's words to us, and they will serve as the criteria upon which we will be judged: whether we have fed the hungry and given drink to the thirsty, welcomed the stranger and clothed the naked, or spent time with the sick and those in prison (see Matthew 25:31–45). Moreover, we will be asked if we have helped others escape the doubt that causes them to fall into despair and which is often a source of loneliness; if we have helped to overcome the ignorance in which millions of people live, especially children deprived of the necessary means to free them from the bonds of poverty; if we have been close to the lonely and afflicted; if we have forgiven those who have offended us and have rejected all forms of anger and hate that lead to violence; if we have had the kind of patience God shows, who is so patient with us; and if we have commended our brothers and sisters to the Lord in prayer. In each of these "little ones," Christ himself is present. His flesh becomes visible in the flesh of the tortured, the crushed, the scourged, the malnourished, and the exiled . . . to be acknowledged, touched, and cared for by us. Let us not forget the words of Saint John of the Cross: "as we prepare to leave this life, we will be judged on the basis of love."

17. Every confessor must accept the faithful as the father in the parable of the prodigal son: a father who runs out to meet his son despite the fact that he has squandered away his inheritance. Confessors are called to embrace the repentant son who comes back home and to express the joy of having him back again. Let us never tire of also going out to the other son who stands outside, incapable of rejoicing, in order to explain to him that his judgment is severe and unjust and meaningless in light of the father's boundless mercy.

May confessors not ask useless questions, but like the father in the parable, interrupt the speech prepared ahead of time by the prodigal son, so that confessors will learn to accept the plea for help and mercy pouring from the heart of every penitent. In short, confessors are called to be a sign of the primacy of mercy always, everywhere, and in every situation, no matter what.

20. The appeal Jesus makes to the text from the book of the prophet Hosea—"I desire love and not sacrifice" (Hosea 6:6)—is important in this regard. Jesus affirms that, from that time onward, the rule of life for his disciples must place mercy at the center, as Jesus himself demonstrated by sharing meals with sinners. Mercy, once again, is revealed as a fundamental aspect of Jesus' mission. This is truly challenging to his hearers, who would draw the line at a formal respect for the law. Jesus, on the other hand, goes beyond the law; the company he keeps with those the law considers sinners makes us realize the depth of his mercy.

The apostle Paul makes a similar journey. Prior to meeting Jesus on the road to Damascus, he dedicated his life to pursuing the justice of the law with zeal (see Philippians 3:6). His conversion to Christ led him to turn that vision upside down, to the point that he would write to the Galatians: "We have believed in Christ Jesus, in order to be justified by faith in Christ, and not by works of the law, because by works of the law shall no one be justified" (Galatians 2:16).

Paul's understanding of justice changes radically. He now places faith first, not justice. Salvation comes not through the observance of the law, but through faith in Jesus Christ, who in his death and resurrection brings salvation together with a mercy that justifies. God's justice now becomes the liberating force for those oppressed by slavery to sin and its consequences. God's justice is his mercy (see Psalm 51:11–16).

21. If God limited himself to only justice, he would cease to be God and would instead be like human beings who ask merely that the law be respected. But mere justice is not enough. Experience shows that an appeal to justice alone will result in its destruction. This is why God goes beyond justice with his mercy and forgiveness. Yet this does not mean that justice should be devalued or rendered superfluous. On the contrary: anyone who makes

a mistake must pay the price. However, this is just the beginning of conversion, not its end, because one begins to feel the tenderness and mercy of God. God does not deny justice. He rather envelopes it and surpasses it with an even greater event in which we experience love as the foundation of true justice. . . . God's justice is his mercy given to everyone as a grace that flows from the death and resurrection of Jesus Christ. Thus the Cross of Christ is God's judgment on all of us and on the whole world, because through it he offers us the certitude of love and new life.

23. There is an aspect of mercy that goes beyond the confines of the Church. It relates us to Judaism and Islam, both of which consider mercy to be one of God's most important attributes. Israel was the first to receive this revelation, which continues in history as the source of an inexhaustible richness meant to be shared with all humanity. As we have seen, the pages of the Old Testament are steeped in mercy, because they narrate the works that the Lord performed in favor of his people at the most trying moments of their history. Among the privileged names that Islam attributes to the Creator are "Merciful and Kind." This invocation is often on the lips of faithful Muslims who feel themselves accompanied and sustained by mercy in their daily weakness. They too believe that no one can place a limit on divine mercy because its doors are always open.

24. At the foot of the Cross, Mary, together with John, the disciple of love, witnessed the words of forgiveness spoken by Jesus. This supreme expression of mercy toward those who crucified him show us the point to which the mercy of God can reach. Mary attests that the mercy of the Son of God knows no bounds and extends to everyone, without exception. Let us address her in the words of the *Salve Regina*, a prayer ever ancient and ever new, so that she may never tire of turning her merciful eyes upon us, and make us worthy to contemplate the face of mercy, her Son Jesus.

# 2

# The Essential Thing Is Mercy

In the Gospel the essential thing is *mercy*. God sent his Son; God made himself man in order to save us—that is, in order to grant us his mercy. Jesus says this clearly, summarizing his teaching for the disciples: "Be merciful, even as your Father is merciful" (Luke 6:36). Can there be a Christian who isn't merciful? No. A Christian must necessarily be merciful, because this is the center of the Gospel. And faithful to this teaching, the Church can only repeat the same thing to her children: "Be merciful," as the Father is, and as Jesus was.

The Church is Mother, by teaching her children works of mercy. She learned this manner from Jesus; she learned that this is what's essential for salvation. It's not enough to love those who love us. Jesus says that pagans do this. It's not enough to do good to those who do good to us. To change the world for the better, it is necessary to do good to those who are not able to return the favor, as the Father has done with us, by giving us Jesus. How much have we paid for our redemption? Nothing, totally free! Doing good without expecting anything in return. This is what the Father did with us, and we must do the same.

Someone might say to me, "But Father, I don't have time," "I have so many things to do," "It's difficult," "What can I do with my feebleness and my sins, with so many things?" We are often satisfied with a few prayers, with a distracted and sporadic participation in Sunday Mass, with a few charitable acts; but we do not have the courage "to come out" to bring Christ to others. We are a bit like St. Peter. As soon as Jesus speaks of his Passion, death, and resurrection, of the gift of himself, of love for all, the apostle takes him aside and reproaches him. What Jesus says upsets Peter's plans, seems unacceptable, and threatens the security he has built for himself, his idea of the Messiah. And Jesus looks at his disciples and addresses to Peter what may possibly be the harshest words in the Gospels: "Get behind me, Satan! For you are not on the side of God, but of men" (Mark 8:33). God always thinks with mercy: do not forget this. God always thinks mercifully. He is the merciful Father!

When we enter our hearts, we find things that aren't okay, things that aren't good, as Jesus found that filth of profiteering . . . in the Temple. Inside of us, too, there are unclean things; there are sins of selfishness, of arrogance, pride, greed, envy, jealousy . . . so many sins! We can even continue the dialogue with Jesus: "Jesus, do you trust me? I want you to trust me. Thus I open the door to you, and you cleanse my soul." Ask the Lord that. As he went to cleanse the Temple, he may come to cleanse your soul. We imagine that he comes with a whip of cords. . . . No, he doesn't cleanse the soul with that! Do you know what kind of whip Jesus uses to cleanse our soul? Mercy. Open your heart to Jesus' mercy! Say, "Jesus, look how much filth! Come, cleanse. Cleanse with your mercy, with your tender words, cleanse with your caresses." If we open our heart to Jesus' mercy, in order to cleanse our heart, our soul, Jesus will trust himself to us.

The Church, which is holy, does not reject sinners; she does not reject us all; she does not reject us because she calls everyone, welcomes them, is open even to those furthest from her. She calls everyone to allow themselves to be enfolded by the mercy, the tenderness, and the forgiveness of the Father, who offers everyone the possibility of meeting him, of journeying toward sanctity. "Well! Father, I am a sinner; I have tremendous sins. How can I possibly feel part of the Church?" Dear brother, dear sister, this is exactly what the Lord wants, that you say to him,

> *The Church, which is holy, does not reject sinners; she does not reject us all; she does not reject us because she calls everyone, welcomes them, is open even to those furthest from her.*

"Lord, here I am, with my sins." Is one of you here without sin? Anyone? No one, not one of us. We all carry our sins with us. But the Lord wants to hear us say to him, "Forgive me, help me to walk, change my heart!" And the Lord can change your heart.

The prophet Hosea says, "I have walked with you, and I taught you how to walk as a father teaches his child to walk." It's beautiful, this image of God! And this is God with us: he teaches us to walk. And it is the same attitude he maintains toward the Church. We, too, despite our resolve to follow the Lord Jesus, experience every day the selfishness and hardness of our heart. When, however, we recognize ourselves as sinners, God fills us with his mercy and with his love. And he forgives us, he always forgives us. And it is precisely this that makes us grow as God's people, as the Church: not our cleverness, not our merits—we are a small thing, it's not that—but the daily experience of how much the Lord wishes us well and takes care of us. It is this that makes us feel that we are truly his, in his hands, and makes us grow in communion with him and with one another. To be Church is to feel oneself in the hands of God, who is father and loves us, caresses us, waits for us, and makes us feel his tenderness.

Dear brothers and sisters, the Lord never tires of having mercy on us, and wants to offer us his forgiveness once again—we all need it—inviting us to return to him with a new heart, purified of evil, purified by tears, to take part in his joy. How should we accept this invitation? St. Paul advises us: "We beseech you on behalf of Christ, be reconciled to God" (2 Cor. 5:20). This power of conversion is not only the work of mankind; it is letting oneself be reconciled. Reconciliation between us and God is possible thanks to the mercy of the Father, who, out of love for us, did not hesitate to sacrifice his only begotten Son. Indeed, Christ, who was just and without sin, was made to be sin (2 Cor. 5:21) when, on the cross, he took on the burden of our sins, and in this way he redeemed and justified us before God. "In him" we can become just, in him we can change, if we accept the grace of God and do not allow this "acceptable time" to pass in vain (2 Cor. 6:2). Please, let us stop, let us stop a while and let ourselves be reconciled to God.

Celebrating the sacrament of reconciliation means being enfolded in a warm embrace; it is the embrace of the Father's infinite mercy. Let us recall that beautiful, beautiful parable of the son who left his home with the money of his inheritance. He wasted all the money and then, when he had nothing left, decided to return home, not as a son but as a servant. His heart was filled with so much guilt and shame. The surprise came when he began to speak, to ask for forgiveness. His father did not let him speak; he embraced him, he kissed him, and he began to make merry. But I am telling you: each time we go to confession, God embraces us. God rejoices! Let us go forward on this road.

In the Church, the God we encounter is not a merciless judge but is like the father in the Gospel parable. You may be like the son who left home, who sank to the depths, furthest from the Gospel. When you have the strength to say "I want to come home," you will find the door open. God will come to meet you because he is always waiting for you. God is always waiting for you, God embraces you, kisses you, and celebrates. That is how the Lord is, that is how the tenderness of our Heavenly Father is.

[The father in the parable] went every day to see if his son was coming home: this is our merciful Father. It indicates that he was waiting for him with longing on the terrace of his house. God thinks like the Samaritan who did not pass by the unfortunate man, pitying him or looking at him from the other side of the road, but helped him without asking for anything in return—without asking whether he was a Jew, a pagan, or a Samaritan, whether he was rich or poor: he asked for nothing. He went to help him; God is like this. God thinks like the shepherd who lays down his life in order to defend and save his sheep.

One might say: I confess only to God. Yes, you can say to God, "forgive me" and confess your sins, but our sins are also committed against the brethren and against the Church. That is why it is necessary to ask pardon of the Church, and of the brethren in the person of the priest. "But Father, I am ashamed . . ." Shame is also good; it is healthy to feel a little shame, because being ashamed is salutary. In my country when a person feels no shame, we say that he is "shameless," a *sinvergüenza*. But shame, too, does good, because it makes us more humble, and the priest receives this confession with love and tenderness and forgives us on God's behalf. Also, from a human point of view, in order to unburden oneself, it is good to talk with a brother and tell the priest these things that are weighing so much on my heart. And one feels that one is unburdening oneself before God, with the Church, with his brother.

The sacrament of reconciliation is a sacrament of healing. When I go to confession, it is to be healed; to heal my soul, to heal my heart, and to be healed of some wrongdoing. The biblical icon that best expresses them in their deep bond is the episode of the forgiving and healing of the paralytic, where the Lord Jesus is revealed at the same time as the physician not only of souls but also of bodies (see Mark 2:1–12; Matt. 9:1–8; Luke 5:17–26).

The forgiveness of our sins is not something we can give ourselves. I cannot say, "I forgive my sins." Forgiveness is asked for, is asked of another, and in confession we ask for forgiveness from Jesus. Forgiveness is not the fruit of our own efforts, but rather it's a gift; it is a gift of the Holy Spirit, who fills us with the wellspring of mercy and of grace that flows unceasingly from the open heart of the crucified and risen Christ. Second, Jesus reminds us that we can truly be at peace only if we allow ourselves to be reconciled, in the Lord Jesus, with the Father and with one another. And we have all felt this in our hearts, when we have gone to confession with a soul weighed down and with a little sadness; when we receive Jesus' forgiveness we feel at peace, with that peace of soul that is so beautiful, and that only Jesus can give, only him.

Jesus gave the apostles the power to forgive sins. It is a little difficult to understand how a man can forgive sins, but Jesus gives this power. *The Church is the depository of the power of the keys*, of opening or closing to forgiveness. God forgives every man in his sovereign mercy, but he himself willed that those who belong to Christ and to the Church receive forgiveness by means of the ministers of the community. Through the apostolic ministry the mercy of God reaches me, my faults are forgiven, and joy is bestowed on me. In this way Jesus calls us to live out reconciliation in the ecclesial—community—dimension as well. And this is very beautiful. The Church, who is holy and at the same time in need of penitence, accompanies us on the journey of conversion throughout life. The Church is not mistress of the power of the keys but a servant of the ministry of mercy, and she rejoices every time she can offer this divine gift.

Do not be afraid of confession! When one is in line to go to confession, one feels all these things, even shame, but then when one finishes confession, one leaves free, grand, beautiful, forgiven, candid, happy. This is the beauty of confession. When was the last time you made your confession? Think about it. . . . Two days, two weeks, two years, twenty years, forty years? If much time has passed, do not lose another day. Go, the priest will be good. Jesus is there, and Jesus is more benevolent than priests. Jesus receives you; he receives you with so much love. Be courageous and go to confession!

Perhaps many do not understand the ecclesial dimension of forgiveness, because individualism and subjectivism always dominate, and even we Christians are affected by this. Certainly, God forgives every penitent sinner, personally, but the Christian is tied to Christ, and Christ is united to the Church. For us Christians there is a further gift; there is also a further duty: to pass humbly through the ecclesial community. We have to appreciate it; it is a gift, a cure, a protection, as well as the assurance that God has forgiven me. I go to my brother priest, and I say: "Father, I did this . . ." And he responds: "But I forgive you; God forgives you." At that moment, I am sure that God has forgiven me! And this is beautiful; this is having the surety that God forgives us always, he never tires of forgiving us. And we must never tire of going to ask for forgiveness.

There is a biblical icon that expresses, in all its depths, the mystery that shines through the anointing of the sick. It is the parable of the good Samaritan contained in the Gospel of Luke (10:30–35). Each time we celebrate this sacrament, the Lord Jesus, in the person of the priest, comes close to the one who suffers who is elderly or seriously ill. The parable says that the good Samaritan takes care of the suffering man by pouring oil and wine on his wounds. Oil makes us think of that which is blessed by the bishop each year at the Holy Thursday Chrism Mass, precisely in view of the anointing of the sick. Wine, however, is a sign of Christ's love and grace, which flow from the gift of his life for us and are expressed in all their richness in the sacramental life of the Church. Finally, the suffering person is entrusted to an innkeeper, so that he might continue to care for him, sparing no expense. Now, who is this innkeeper? It is the Church, the Christian community—it is us—to whom each day the Lord entrusts those who are afflicted in body and spirit, so that we might lavish all of his mercy and salvation upon them without measure.

This mandate is repeated in an explicit and precise manner in the letter of James (5:14–15), where he recommends: "Is any among you sick? Let him call for the elders of the church, and let them pray over him, anointing him with oil in the name of the Lord; and the prayer of faith will save the sick man, and the Lord will raise him up; and if he has committed sins, he will be forgiven." It was therefore a practice that was already taking place at the time of the apostles. Jesus in fact taught his disciples to have the same preferential love that he did for the sick and suffering, and he transmitted to them the ability and duty to continue providing, in his name and after his own heart, relief and peace through the special grace of this sacrament. This, however, should not make us fall into an obsessive search for miracles or the presumption that one can always and in any situation be healed. Rather, it is the reassurance of Jesus' closeness to the sick and the aged, too, because any elderly person, anyone over the age of sixty-five, can receive this sacrament, through which Jesus himself draws close to us.

But when someone is sick, and we say, "Let's call for the priest to come," sometimes we think, *No, then he will bring bad luck, let's not call him,* or *He will scare the sick person.* Why do we think this? Because the idea is floating about that the undertakers arrive after the priest. And this is not true. The priest comes to help the sick or elderly person; that is why the priest's visit to the sick is so important. We ought to call the priest to the sick person's side and say, "Come, give him the anointing, bless him." It is Jesus himself who comes to relieve the sick person, to give him strength, to give him hope, to help him, and also to forgive his sins. And this is very beautiful! And we must not think that this is taboo, because in time of pain and illness it is always good to know that we are not alone. The priest and those who are present during the anointing of the sick, in fact, represent the entire Christian community that as one body huddles around the one who suffers and also around her family, nurturing their faith and hope, and supporting them through their prayers and fraternal warmth.

But the greatest comfort comes from the fact that it is the Lord Jesus who makes himself present in the sacrament, who takes us by the hand, who caresses us as he did with the sick, and who reminds us that we already belong to him and that nothing—not even evil and death—can ever separate us from him. Are we in the habit of calling for the priest so that he might come to our sick—I am not speaking about those who are sick with the flu, for three or four days, but rather about a serious illness—and our elderly, and give them this sacrament, this comfort, this strength of Jesus to continue on? Let us do so!

And I tell you, truly: it grieves me when I come across people who no longer confess because they have been beaten and scolded. They have felt as though the Church doors were being closed in their faces! Please, do not do this: mercy, mercy! The Good Shepherd enters through the door, and the doors of mercy are the wounds of the Lord; if you do not enter into your ministry through the Lord's wounds, you will not be good shepherds.

They all have something in common with us: they are images of God; they are children of God. [We must be] going out to meet everyone, without losing sight of our own position. There is another important point: encountering the poor. If we step outside ourselves, we find poverty. Today—it sickens the heart to say so—the discovery of a tramp who has died of the cold is not news. Today what counts as news is, maybe, a scandal. A scandal—ah, that is news! Today, the thought that a great many children do not have food to eat is not news. This is serious; this is serious! We cannot put up with this! Yet that is how things are. We cannot become starched Christians, those overeducated Christians who speak of theological matters as they calmly sip their tea. No! We must become courageous Christians and go in search of the people who are the very flesh of Christ—those who are the flesh of Christ!

If one understands his brother . . . he loves his brother, because he forgives; he understands, he forgives, he is patient. . . . Is this love or hate? We must be sure of this. And we must ask the Lord for two graces. The first: to know what is in our own heart, not to deceive ourselves, not to live in deceit. The second grace: to do what is good in our hearts and not to do the evil that is in our hearts. And as for "killing," remember that words can kill. Even ill will toward another kills. Often, when we listen to people talking, saying evil things about others, it seems like the sin of slander. The sin of defamation had been removed from the Ten Commandments, and yet to speak evil of a person is still a sin. Why is speaking ill of another a sin? Because there is hatred in my heart, aversion, not love. We must always ask for this grace: to know what is happening in our heart, to constantly make the right choice, the choice for good. And that the Lord help us to love one another. And if I cannot love another well, why not? Pray for that person, pray that the Lord make me love him. And like this we move forward, remembering that what taints our lives is the evil that comes from our hearts. And that the Lord can help us.

Think of the gossip [among Jesus' followers] after he called Matthew: he associates with sinners (see Mark 2:16)! He comes for us, when we recognize that we are sinners. But if we are like the Pharisee before the altar, who said, "I thank you, Lord, that I am not like other men, and especially not like the one at the door, like that publican" (see Luke 18:11–12), then we do not know the Lord's heart, and we will never have the joy of experiencing this mercy! It is not easy to entrust oneself to God's mercy, because it is an abyss beyond our comprehension. But we must! "Oh, Father, if you knew my life, you would not say that to me!" "Why, what have you done?" "Oh, I am a great sinner!" "All the better! Go to Jesus: he likes you to tell him these things!" Jesus forgets—he has a very special capacity for forgetting. He forgets, he kisses you, he embraces you, and he simply says to you, "Neither do I condemn you; go, and sin no more" (John 8:11). That is the only advice he gives you. After a month, if we are in the same situation . . . let us go back to the Lord. The Lord never tires of forgiving: never! It is we who tire of asking his forgiveness. Let us ask for the grace not to tire of asking forgiveness, because he never tires of forgiving. Let us ask for this grace.

I would like to emphasize one other thing: God's patience has to call forth in us the *courage to return to him*, however many mistakes and sins there may be in our lives. Jesus tells Thomas to put his hand in the wounds of his hands and his feet and in his side. We too can enter into the wounds of Jesus; we can actually touch him. This happens every time we receive the sacraments with faith. St. Bernard, in a fine homily, said: "Through the wounds of Jesus I can suck honey from the rock and oil from the flinty rock (see Deut. 32:13), I can taste and see the goodness of the Lord" (*On the Song of Songs* 61:4). It is there, in the wounds of Jesus, that we are truly secure; there we encounter the boundless love of his heart. Thomas understood this. St. Bernard goes on to ask: But what can I count on? My own merits? No. "My merit is God's mercy. I am by no means lacking merits as long as he is rich in mercy. If the mercies of the Lord are manifold, I too will abound in merits" (61:5).

This is important: the courage to trust in Jesus' mercy, to trust in his patience, to seek refuge always in the wounds of his love. St. Bernard even stated: "So what if my conscience gnaws at me for my many sins? 'Where sin has abounded, there grace has abounded all the more' (Rom. 5:20)" (61:5). Maybe someone among us here is thinking, *My sin is so great, I am as far from God as the younger son in the parable; my unbelief is like that of Thomas. I don't have the courage to go back, to believe that God can welcome me and that he is waiting for me, of all people.* But God is indeed waiting for you; he asks of you only the courage to go to him. How many times in my pastoral ministry have I heard it said, "Father, I have many sins"? And I have always pleaded, "Don't be afraid, go to him, he is waiting for you, he will take care of everything."

We hear many offers from the world around us; but let us take up God's offer instead: his is a caress of love. For God, we are not numbers, we are important; indeed we are the most important thing to him. Even if we are sinners, we are what is closest to his heart.

Jesus challenges us . . . to take seriously his approach to life and to decide which path is right for us and leads to true joy. This is the great challenge of faith. Jesus was not afraid to ask his disciples if they truly wanted to follow him or if they preferred to take another path (see John 6:67). Simon Peter had the courage to reply, "Lord, to whom shall we go? You have the words of eternal life" (John 6:68). If you, too, are able to say yes to Jesus, your lives will become both meaningful and fruitful.

# 3

# God's Patience toward Us

The origin of the darkness that envelops the world is lost in the night of the ages. Let us think back to that dark moment when the first crime of humanity was committed, when the hand of Cain, blinded by envy, killed his brother Abel (see Gen. 4:8). As a result, the unfolding of the centuries has been marked by violence, wars, hatred, and oppression. But God, who placed a sense of expectation within us, who are made in his image and likeness, was waiting. God was waiting. He waited for so long that perhaps at a certain point it seemed he should have given up. But he could not give up because he could not deny himself (see 2 Tim. 2:13). Therefore, he continued to wait patiently in the face of the corruption of humanity and peoples. The patience of God. How difficult it is to comprehend this: God's patience toward us.

In the Bible, God always appears as the one who takes the initiative in the encounter with humanity. It is he who seeks man, and usually he seeks him precisely while man is in the bitter and tragic moment of betraying God and fleeing from him. God does not wait to seek him; he seeks him out immediately. He is a patient seeker, our Father! He goes before us and waits for us always. He never tires of waiting for us; he is never far from us, but he has the patience to wait for the best moment to meet each one of us. And when the encounter happens, it is never rushed, because God wants to remain at length with us to sustain us, to console us, to give us his joy. God hastens to meet us, but he never rushes to leave us. He stays with us. As we long for him and desire him, so he too desires to be with us, that we may belong to him.

We are his "belonging," we are his creatures. We can say that God thirsts for us, to meet us. Our God is thirsty for us. And this is God's heart.

The Word of God pitched his tent among us, sinners who are in need of mercy. And we all must hasten to receive the grace he offers us. Instead, the Gospel of St. John continues, "his own people received him not" (1:11). We reject him too many times, we prefer to remain closed in our errors and the anxiety of our sins. But Jesus does not desist and never ceases to offer himself and his grace, which saves us! Jesus is patient; he knows how to wait, and he waits for us always. This is a message of hope, a message of salvation, ancient and ever new. And we are called to witness with joy to this message of the Gospel of life, to the Gospel of light, of hope, and of love. For Jesus' message is this: life, light, hope, and love.

Jesus is all mercy. Jesus is all love: he is God made man. Each one of us is that little lost lamb, the coin that was mislaid; each one of us is that son who has squandered his freedom on false idols, illusions of happiness, and has lost everything. But God does not forget us; the Father never abandons us. He is a patient father, always waiting for us! He respects our freedom, but he remains faithful forever. And when we come back to him, he welcomes us like children into his house, for he never ceases, not for one instant, to wait for us with love. And his heart rejoices over every child who returns. He is celebrating because he is joy. God has this joy, when one of us sinners goes to him and asks his forgiveness.

[Remember] Peter: three times he denied Jesus, precisely when he should have been closest to him; and when he hits bottom he meets the gaze of Jesus, who patiently, wordlessly, says to him, "Peter, don't be afraid of your weakness, trust in me." Peter understands, he feels the loving gaze of Jesus, and he weeps. How beautiful is this gaze of Jesus—how much tenderness is there! Brothers and sisters, let us never lose trust in the patience and mercy of God!

Jesus, when on the cross, heard them challenging him: "Come down, come down!" Patient until the end, because he has patience with us. He always enters, he is involved with us, but he does so in his own way and when he thinks it's best. He tells us exactly what [the Lord] told Abraham: Walk in my presence and be blameless, be above reproach. This is exactly the right word. Walk in my presence and try to be above reproach. This is the journey with the Lord, and he intervenes, but we have to wait, wait for the moment, walking always in his presence and trying to be beyond reproach. We ask this grace from the Lord, to walk always in his presence, trying to be blameless.

The Gospel presents to us the episode of the adulterous woman (John 8:1–11), whom Jesus saves from being condemned to death. Jesus' attitude is striking: we do not hear words of scorn, we do not hear words of condemnation, but only words of love and of mercy, which are an invitation to conversion. "Neither do I condemn you; go, and do not sin again" (John 8:11). Ah! Brothers and sisters, God's face is the face of a merciful father who is always patient. Have you thought about God's patience, the patience he has with each one of us? That is his mercy. He always has patience—patience with us. He understands us, he waits for us, he does not tire of forgiving us if we are able to return to him with a contrite heart. "Great is God's mercy," says the psalm.

[T]he apostle Thomas personally experiences [the] mercy of God, which has a concrete face: the face of Jesus, the risen Jesus. Thomas does not believe it when the other apostles tell him, "We have seen the Lord." It isn't enough for him that Jesus had foretold it, promised it: "On the third day I will rise." He wants to see, he wants to put his hand in the place of the nails and in Jesus' side. And how does Jesus react? With *patience*: Jesus does not abandon Thomas in his stubborn unbelief; he gives him a week's time. He does not close the door; he waits. And Thomas acknowledges his own poverty, his little faith: "My Lord and my God!" With this simple yet faith-filled invocation, he responds to Jesus' patience. He lets himself be enveloped by divine mercy; he sees it before his eyes, in the wounds of Christ's hands and feet and in his open side, and he discovers trust. He is a new man, no longer an unbeliever, but a believer.

Let us think too of the two disciples on the way to Emmaus: their sad faces, their barren journey, their despair. But Jesus does not abandon them:

he walks beside them, and not only that! Patiently he explains the Scriptures that spoke of him, and he stays to share a meal with them. This is God's way of doing things: he is not impatient like us, who often want everything all at once, even in our dealings with other people. God is patient with us because he loves us, and those who love are able to understand, to hope, to inspire confidence. They do not give up, they do not burn bridges; they are able to forgive. Let us remember this in our lives as Christians: God always waits for us, even when we have left him behind! He is never far from us, and if we return to him, he is ready to embrace us.

Our lives are sometimes similar to that of the blind man who opened himself to the light, who opened himself to God, who opened himself to God's grace. Sometimes, unfortunately, our lives are similar to that of the doctors of the law: from the height of our pride we judge others, and even the Lord! Today, we are invited to open ourselves to the light of Christ in order to bear fruit in our lives, to eliminate un-Christian behaviors; we are all Christians, but everyone sometimes has un-Christian behaviors—that is, behaviors that are sins. We must repent of this, eliminate these behaviors in order to journey well along the way of holiness, which has its origin in baptism. We, too, have been "enlightened" by Christ in baptism, so that, as St. Paul reminds us, we may act as "children of light" (Eph. 5:8), with humility, patience, and mercy.

The liturgy proposes several Gospel parables—that is, short stories Jesus used to announce to the crowds the Kingdom of Heaven. Among those stories is a rather complex one that Jesus explained to the disciples: that of the good grain and the weed, a story that deals with the problem of evil in the world and calls attention to God's patience (see Matt. 13:24–30, 36–43). The story takes place in a field where the owner sows grain, but during the night his enemy comes and sows "weed," a term that in Hebrew derives from the same root as the name *Satan* and that alludes to the concept of division. We all know that the demon is a "sower of weed," one who always seeks to sow division between individuals, families, nations, and peoples. The servants wanted to uproot the weed immediately, but the field owner stopped them, explaining that "in gathering the weeds you root up the wheat along with them" (Matt. 13:29). Because we all know that a weed, when it grows, looks very much like good grain, and there is the risk of confusing them.

The teaching of the parable is twofold. First of all, it tells us that the evil in the world *comes not from God but from his enemy, the evil one*. It is curious that the evil one goes at night to sow weed, in the dark, in confusion; he goes where there is no light to sow this confusion and division. This enemy is astute: he sows evil in the middle of good; thus it is impossible for us to distinctly separate them. But God, in the end, will be able to do so.

And here we arrive at the second theme: the juxtaposition of the impatience of the servants and the *patient waiting* of the field owner, who represents God. At times we are in a great hurry to judge, to categorize, to put the good here and the bad there. . . . But remember the prayer of that self-righteous man: "God, I thank you that I am good, that I am not like other men, malicious" (see Luke 18:11–12). God, however, knows how to wait.

With patience and mercy he gazes into the "field" of every person's life. He sees much better than we do the filth and the evil, but he also sees the seeds of good and waits with trust for them to grow. God knows how to wait. This is so beautiful: our God is a patient father, who always waits for us and waits with his heart in hand to welcome us, to forgive us. He always forgives us if we go to him.

The field owner's attitude is that of hope grounded in the certainty that evil does not have the first nor the last word. And it is thanks to this *patient hope* of God that the same weed, which is the malicious heart with so many sins, can become good grain in the end. But be careful: evangelical patience is not indifference to evil—we must not confuse good and evil! In facing weeds in the world, the Lord's disciple is called to imitate the patience of God, to nourish hope with the support of indestructible trust in the final victory of good—that is, the victory of God.

In the end, in fact, evil will be removed and eliminated: at the time of harvest—that is, of judgment—the harvesters will follow the orders of the field owner, separating the weed to burn it (see Matt. 13:30). On the day of the final harvest, *the judge will be Jesus*, he who has sown good grain in the world and who himself became the "grain of wheat" who died and rose. In the end we will all be judged by the same measure with which we have judged: *the mercy we have shown to others will also be shown to us*. Let us ask Our Lady, our Mother, to help us to grow in patience, in hope, and in mercy with all brothers and sisters.

The Lord always chooses his way to enter our lives. Often he does so slowly, so slowly that we are in danger of losing our patience a little. *But Lord, when? And we pray. . . .* Or when we think of what the Lord has promised us, that it such a huge thing, we do not believe it, and we are somewhat skeptical, as Abraham was. Yes, there was a bit of skepticism: *What, me? I am almost a hundred years old—how will I and my wife of ninety have a son?*

The Lord takes his time. But even he, in this relationship with us, has a lot of patience. He waits for us. And he waits for us until the end of life! Think of the good thief, on the cross next to Jesus' cross. Right at the end, at the very end, he acknowledged God. The Lord walks with us but often does not reveal himself, as in the case of the disciples of Emmaus. The Lord is involved in our lives—that's for sure!—but often we do not see. This demands our patience. But the Lord who walks with us also has a lot of patience with us.

> The Lord always chooses his way to enter our lives. Often he does so slowly, so slowly that we are in danger of losing our patience a little. But Lord, when?

God asks us for faithfulness and patience. Faithfulness like that of Daniel, who was faithful to his God and who worshipped him to the end. And patience, because every hair on your head is counted, as the Lord has promised.

[Listening] always demands the patience of one who knows full well what St. Thomas Aquinas tells us: anyone can have grace and charity and yet falter in the exercise of the virtues because of persistent "contrary inclinations." In other words, the organic unity of the virtues always and necessarily exists *in habitu*, even though forms of conditioning can hinder the operations of those virtuous habits. Hence the need for "a pedagogy that will introduce people step by step to the full appropriation of the mystery." Reaching a level of maturity in which individuals can make truly free and responsible decisions calls for much time and patience. As [St.] Peter Faber used to say: "Time is God's messenger."

"The Lord who walks with God is also the Lord of patience": the patience "which he had with all these generations, with all these people who lived their history of grace and sin." "God is patient, God walks with us, because he wants all of us to come to be conformed to the image of his Son." "From that moment in Creation in which he gave us freedom—not independence—until today, he continues to journey."

And above all, a love that is patient: patience is a virtue of God, and he teaches us how to cultivate it in family life, how to be patient, and lovingly so, with one another. To be patient among ourselves. A patient love. God alone knows how to create harmony from differences. But if God's love is lacking, the family loses its harmony, self-centeredness prevails, and joy fades. But the family that experiences the joy of faith communicates it naturally. That family is the salt of the earth and the light of the world; it is the leaven of society as a whole.

"But, father, I work in a factory; I work as an accountant, only with numbers; you can't be a saint there." Yes, yes you can! There, where you work, you can become a saint. God gives you the grace to become holy. God communicates himself to you. Always, in every place, one can become a saint—that is, one can open oneself to this grace, which works inside us and leads us to holiness. Are you a parent or a grandparent? Be a saint by passionately teaching your children or grandchildren to know and to follow Jesus. And it takes so much patience to do this: to be a good parent, a good grandfather, a good mother, a good grandmother. It requires so much patience, and by exercising patience we come to holiness. Are you a catechist, an educator, or a volunteer? Be a saint by becoming a visible sign of God's love and presence alongside us. This is it: every state of life leads to holiness, always! In your home, on the street, at work, at church, in that moment and in your state of life, the path to sainthood has been opened. Don't be discouraged from pursuing this path. It is God alone who gives us the grace. The Lord asks only this: that we be in communion with him and at the service of our brothers and sisters.

God's love always comes before our own! He always takes the initiative. He waits for us, he invites us, and the initiative is always his. Jesus is God made man, made flesh; he is born for us. The new star that appeared to the Magi was a sign of the birth of Christ. Had they not seen the star, these men would not have set out. The light goes before us, truth goes before us, and beauty precedes us. God goes before us. The prophet Isaiah said that God is like the flower of the almond tree. Why? Because in that region the almond is the first to flower. And God goes ever before us. He is always the first to seek us, he takes the first step. God goes ever before us. His grace precedes us and this grace appeared in Jesus. *He is the Epiphany.* He, Jesus Christ, is the manifestation of God's love. With us.

# 4

# Jesus Is Risen! We Have Seen Him!

The dominant sentiment that shines forth from the Gospel accounts of the Resurrection is joy full of wonder, but a great wonder! Joy that comes from within! And in the liturgy we relive the state of mind of the disciples over the news the women had brought: Jesus is risen! We have seen him!

All divine revelation is the fruit of the dialogue between God and his people, and even faith in the Resurrection is tied to this dialogue, which accompanies the journey of the People of God in history. It is not surprising that a mystery so great, so decisive, so superhuman as that of the Resurrection, required the whole journey, all the time necessary, up to Jesus Christ. He can say, "I am the resurrection and the life" (John 11:25), because in him this mystery is not only revealed in its fullness but takes place, happens, and becomes, for the first time and forever, reality. The Gospel we have heard—the account of the death of Jesus and that of the empty tomb—represents the culmination of that entire journey. The event of the Resurrection answers the long search of the People of God, the search of every person and of the whole of humanity.

[In] the profession of faith in the New Testament, only men are recorded as witnesses of the Resurrection, the apostles, but not the women. This is because, according to the Judaic law of that time, women and children could not bear a trustworthy, credible witness. Instead, in the Gospels women play a fundamental lead role. Here we can grasp an element in favor of the historicity of the Resurrection: if it were an invented event, in the context of that time it would not have been linked to the evidence of women. Instead, the Evangelists simply recounted what happened: women were the first witnesses. This implies that God does not choose in accordance with human criteria. The first witnesses of Jesus' birth were shepherds—simple, humble people; the first witnesses of the Resurrection were women. And this is beautiful. This is part of the mission of women! Witnessing to their children and to their grandchildren, that Jesus is alive, is living, is risen. Mothers and women, carry on witnessing to this! It is the heart that counts for God: how open to him we are, whether we are like trusting children.

But let us return to the Gospel, to the women, and take one step further. They find the tomb empty, the body of Jesus not there; something new has happened, but all this still doesn't tell them anything certain. Rather, it raises questions; it leaves them confused, without offering an answer. And suddenly there are two men in dazzling clothes who say, "Why do you look for the living among the dead? He is not here; but has risen" (Luke 24:5–6). What was a simple act, done surely out of love—going to the tomb—has now turned into an event, a truly life-changing event. Nothing remains as it was before, not only in the lives of those women but also in our own lives and in the history of humankind.

*All divine revelation is the fruit of the dialogue between God and his people, and even faith in the Resurrection is tied to this dialogue, which accompanies the journey of the People of God in history.*

After his appearances to the women, other appearances follow. Jesus makes himself present in a new way: he is the Crucified One but his body is glorified. He did not return to earthly life but returned in a new condition. At first they do not recognize him, and it is only through his words and gestures that their eyes are opened. The meeting with the Risen One transforms; it gives to faith fresh strength and a steadfast foundation.

Jesus is not dead, he has risen, he is *alive*! He does not simply return to life; rather, he is life itself, because he is the Son of God, *the living God* (see Num. 14:21–28; Deut. 5:26; Josh. 3:10). Jesus no longer belongs to the past but lives in the present and is projected toward the future; Jesus is the everlasting "today" of God. This is how the newness of God appears to the women, the disciples, and all of us: as victory over sin, evil, and death—over everything that crushes life and makes it seem less human.

We need to hear ourselves repeat the angels' admonition and to remind one another of it. This admonition: "Why do you seek the living among the dead?" helps us leave behind our empty sadness and opens us to the horizons of joy and hope. That hope, which rolls back the stones from tombs and encourages us to proclaim the Good News, is capable of generating new life for others. Let us repeat the angels' phrase in order to keep it in our hearts and in our memory, and then let everyone respond in silence: "Why do you seek the living among the dead?" Let's repeat it! . . . Behold, brothers and sisters, he is alive, he is with us! Do not go to the many tombs that today promise you something . . . and then give you nothing! He is alive! Let us not now seek the living among the dead!

And this is a message meant for me and for you, dear sister, for you, dear brother. How often does Love have to tell us, "Why do you look for the living among the dead?" Our daily problems and worries can wrap us up in ourselves, in sadness and bitterness . . . and that is where death is. That is not the place to look for the One who is alive! Let the risen Jesus enter your life—welcome him as a friend, with trust: he is life! If up till now you have kept him at a distance, step forward. He will receive you with open arms. If you have been indifferent, take a risk; you won't be disappointed. If following him seems difficult, don't be afraid. Trust him, be confident that he is close to you, that he is with you, and he will give you the peace you are looking for and the strength to live as he would have you do.

John's Gospel tells us that Jesus appeared twice to the apostles enclosed in the Upper Room: the first time on the evening of the Resurrection itself, and on that occasion Thomas, who said, "Unless I see and touch I will not believe," was absent. The second time, eight days later, Thomas was there as well. And Jesus said, speaking directly to him, I invite you to look at my wounds, to touch them; then Thomas exclaimed, "My Lord and my God!" (John 20:28). So Jesus said, "Have you believed because you have seen me? Blessed are those who have not seen and yet believe" (John 20:29). And who were those who believed without seeing? Other disciples, other men and women of Jerusalem, who, on the testimony of the apostles and the women, believed, even though they had not met the risen Jesus. This is a very important word about faith—we can call it *the beatitude of faith*. Blessed are those who have not seen but have believed: this is the beatitude of faith! In every epoch and in every place blessed are those who, on the strength of the Word of God proclaimed in the Church and witnessed by Christians, believe that Jesus Christ is the love of God incarnate, mercy incarnate. And this applies for each one of us!

Jesus, in the New Testament . . . ties faith in the resurrection to his own person and says, "I am the resurrection and the life" (John 11:25). It will be our Lord Jesus who on the last day raises those who have believed in him. Jesus has come among us; he became man like us in all things, except sin; in this way he took us with him on his return journey to the Father. He, the Word Incarnate, who died for us and rose again, gives to his disciples the Holy Spirit as a pledge of full communion in his glorious kingdom, which we vigilantly await. This waiting is the source and reason for our hope, a hope that, if cultivated and guarded—our hope, if we cultivate and guard it—becomes a light that illumines our common history. Let us remember it always: we are disciples of the One who came, who comes every day, and who will come at the end. If we can manage to be more aware of this reality, we will be less fatigued by daily life, less prisoners of the ephemeral and more disposed to walk with a merciful heart on the way of salvation.

What does it mean for the Church, for us today, to be disciples of Jesus, the Lamb of God? It means replacing malice with innocence, replacing power with love, replacing pride with humility, replacing status with service. It is good work! We Christians must do this: replace malice with innocence, replace power with love, replace pride with humility, replace status with service. Being disciples of the Lamb means not living like a "besieged citadel" but like a city placed on a hill, open, welcoming, and supportive. It means not assuming closed attitudes but rather proposing the gospel to everyone, bearing witness by our lives that following Jesus makes us freer and more joyous.

It is not easy to be open to Jesus. Nor is it a given that we shall accept the life of the Risen One and his presence among us. The Gospel shows us different reactions: that of the apostle Thomas, that of Mary Magdalene, and that of the two disciples of Emmaus: it does us good to compare ourselves to them. Thomas places a condition on belief, asking to touch the evidence, the wounds; Mary Magdalene weeps, seeing Jesus but not recognizing him—she realizes it is Jesus only when he calls her by name; the disciples of Emmaus, who are depressed and feeling defeated, attain an encounter with Jesus by allowing that mysterious wayfarer to accompany them. Each one on a different path! They were seeking the living among the dead, and it was the Lord himself who redirected their courses. And what do I do? What route do I take to encounter the living Christ? He will always be close to us to correct our course if we have strayed.

*What does it mean to rise again?* The resurrection of us all will take place on the last day, at the end of the world, through the omnipotence of God, who will return life to our bodies by reuniting them to our souls, through the power of Jesus' resurrection. This is the fundamental explanation: because Jesus rose, we will rise; we have the hope of resurrection because he has opened to us the door of resurrection. And this transformation, this transfiguration of our bodies, is prepared for in this life by our relationship with Jesus, in the sacraments, especially in the Eucharist. We, who are nourished in this life by his Body and by his Blood shall rise again like him, with him, and through him. As Jesus rose with his own body but did not return to this earthly life, so we will be raised again with our own bodies, which will be transfigured into glorified bodies. This is not a lie! This is true. We believe that Jesus is risen, that Jesus is living at this moment. But do you believe that Jesus is alive? And if Jesus is alive, do you think that he will let us die and not make us rise? No! He is waiting for us, and because he is risen, the power of his resurrection will raise us all.

Without this faith in the death and resurrection of Jesus, our hope would be weak. But it would not even be hope. More precisely, the death and resurrection of Jesus are the heart of our hope. The apostle said, "If Christ has not been raised, your faith is futile and you are still in your sins" (1 Cor. 15:17). Unfortunately, some have tried to blur faith in the resurrection of Jesus, and doubts have crept in, even among believers. It is a little like that "rosewater" faith, as we say; it is not a strong faith. And this is due to superficiality and sometimes to indifference, busy as we are with a thousand things considered more important than faith, or because we have a view of life that is solely horizontal. However, it is the Resurrection itself that opens us to greater hope, for it opens our life and the life of the world to the eternal future of God, to full happiness, to the certainty that evil, sin, and death may be overcome. And this leads to living daily situations with greater trust, to facing them with courage and determination. Christ's resurrection illuminates these every-day situations with a new light. The resurrection of Christ is our strength!

The women encounter the newness of God. Jesus has risen, he is alive! But faced with the empty tomb and the two men in brilliant clothes, their first reaction is one of fear: "they were terrified and bowed their faced to the ground," St. Luke tells us—they didn't even have courage to look. But when they hear the message of the Resurrection, they accept it in faith. And the two men in dazzling clothes tell them something of crucial importance: *remember*. "Remember what he told you when he was still in Galilee. . . . And they remembered his words" (Luke 24:6, 8). This is the invitation to *remember* their encounter with Jesus, to remember his words, his actions, his life; and it is precisely this loving remembrance of their experience with the Master that enables the women to master their fear and to bring the message of the resurrection to the apostles and all the others (see Luke 24:9). To remember what God has done and continues to do for me, for us, to remember the road we have traveled—this is what opens our hearts to hope for the future. May we learn to remember everything that God has done in our lives.

Let us allow this experience, which is inscribed in the Gospel, also to be imprinted in our hearts and shine forth from our lives. Let us allow the joyous wonder of Easter Sunday to shine forth in our thoughts, glances, behavior, gestures, and words. . . . If only we were so luminous! But this is not just cosmetic! It comes from within, from a heart immersed in the source of this joy, like that of Mary Magdalene, who wept over the loss of her Lord and could hardly believe her eyes seeing him risen.

Whoever experiences this becomes a witness of the Resurrection, for in a certain sense he himself has risen, she herself has risen. He or she is then capable of carrying a "ray" of light of the Risen One into various situations: to those who are happy, making them more beautiful by preserving them from egoism; to those who are hurting, bringing serenity and hope.

After the death of the Master, the disciples had scattered, their faith been utterly shaken. Everything seemed over, all their certainties had crumbled and their hopes had died. But now that message of the women, incredible as it was, came to them like a ray of light in the darkness. The news spread: Jesus is risen, just as he said. And then there was his command to go to Galilee; the women had heard it twice, first from the angel and then from Jesus himself: "Let them go to Galilee; there they will see me." "Do not fear" and "Go to Galilee."

Galilee is the place where they were first called, where everything began! The apostles were to return there, to the place where they were originally called. Jesus had walked along the shores of the lake as the fishermen were casting their nets. He had called them, and they left everything and followed him (see Matt. 4:18–22).

To return to Galilee means to reread everything on the basis of the cross and its victory, fearlessly: "do not be afraid." To reread everything—Jesus' preaching, his miracles, the new community, the excitement and the defections, even the betrayal—to reread everything starting from the end, which is a new beginning, from this supreme act of love.

For each of us, too, there is a Galilee at the origin of our journey with Jesus. "To go to Galilee" means something beautiful, it means rediscovering our baptism as a living fountainhead, drawing new energy from the sources of our faith and our Christian experience. To return to Galilee means above all to return to that blazing light with which God's grace touched me at the start of the journey. From that flame I can light a fire for today and every day, and bring heat and light to my brothers and sisters. That flame ignites a humble joy, a joy that sorrow and distress cannot dismay. A good, gentle joy.

In the life of every Christian, after baptism there is also another "Galilee," a more existential Galilee: the experience of a *personal encounter with Jesus Christ*, who called me to follow him and to share in his mission. In this sense, returning to Galilee means treasuring in my heart the living memory of that call, when Jesus passed my way, gazed at me with mercy, and asked me to follow him. To return there means reviving the memory of that moment when his eyes met mine, the moment when he made me realize that he loved me.

Today, tonight, each of us can ask: *What is my Galilee?* I need to remind myself, to go back and remember. *Where is my Galilee?* Do I remember it? Have I forgotten it? Seek and you will find it! There the Lord is waiting for you. Have I gone off on roads and paths that made me forget it? Lord, help me: tell me what my Galilee is, for you know that I want to return there to encounter you and to let myself be embraced by your mercy. Do not be afraid, do not fear, return to Galilee!

The Gospel is very clear: we need to go back there, to see Jesus risen, and to become witnesses of his resurrection. This is not to go back in time; it is not a kind of nostalgia. It is returning to our first love, in order to *receive the fire* Jesus has kindled in the world and to bring that fire to all people, to the very ends of the earth. Go back to Galilee, without fear!

"Galilee of the Gentiles" (Matt. 4:15; Isa. 8:23)! Horizon of the risen Lord, horizon of the Church; intense desire of encounter. . . . Let us be on our way!

# 5

# Our Joy Is Jesus Christ

Dear friends, be glad! Do not be afraid of being joyful! Don't be afraid of joy—that joy the Lord gives us when we allow him to enter our lives. Let us allow him to enter our lives and invite us to go out to the margins of life and proclaim the Gospel. Don't be afraid of joy. Have joy and courage!

The human heart desires joy. We all desire joy; every family, every people, aspires to happiness. But what is the joy that the Christian is called to live out and bear witness to? It is the joy that comes from the *closeness of God*, from his *presence* in our life. From the moment Jesus entered history, with his birth in Bethlehem, humanity received the seed of the Kingdom of God, as the soil receives the seed, the promise of a future harvest. There is no need to look further.

Jesus has come to bring joy to all people for all time. It is not just a hopeful joy or a joy postponed until paradise, as if here on earth we are sad but in paradise we will be filled with joy. No! It is not that, but a joy already real and tangible now, because *Jesus himself is our joy*, and with Jesus joy finds its home . . . joy is at home in Jesus. And without Jesus is there joy? No! He is living, he is the Risen One, and he works in us and among us especially with the Word and the sacraments.

The prophet Isaiah (40:1–5) addresses people who have passed through a dark period, who have been subjected to a very difficult trial; but now the time of comfort has come. Sorrow and fear can be replaced with joy, for the Lord himself will guide his people on the way to liberation and salvation. How will he do all this? With the solicitude and tenderness of a shepherd who takes care of his flock. He will in fact provide unity and security and feed his flock, gather the lost sheep into his sure fold, reserve special attention for the most fragile and weak. This is God's attitude toward us, his creatures. For this reason, the prophet invites those who hear him—including us, today—to spread this message of hope: that the Lord consoles us. And to make room for the comfort that comes from the Lord.

Let Isaiah's call—"Comfort, comfort my people"—resound in our hearts. Today there is need for people to be witnesses to the mercy and tenderness of God, who spurs the resigned, enlivens the disheartened, and ignites the fire of hope. He ignites the fire of hope! We don't. So many situations require our comforting witness, to be joyful, comforting people. I am thinking of those who are burdened by suffering, injustice, and tyranny; of those who are slaves to money, to power, to success, to worldliness. Poor dears! They have fabricated consolation, not the true comfort of the Lord! We are all called to comfort our brothers and sisters, to testify that God alone can eliminate the causes of existential and spiritual tragedies. He can do it! He is powerful!

Christian joy, like hope, is founded on God's fidelity, on the certainty that he always keeps his promises. The prophet Isaiah exhorts those who have lost their way and have lost heart to entrust themselves to the faithfulness of the Lord, for his salvation will not delay in bursting into their lives. All those who have encountered Jesus along the way experience a serenity and joy in their hearts that nothing and no one can take away. Our joy is Jesus Christ; his faithful love is inexhaustible. Therefore, when a Christian becomes sad, it means that he has distanced himself from Jesus. But then we must not leave him alone! We should pray for him and make him feel the warmth of the community.

[The] joy of the Gospel is not just any joy. It consists in knowing one is welcomed and loved by God. As the prophet Isaiah reminds us, God is he who comes to save us and who seeks to help, especially those who are fearful of heart. His coming among us strengthens us, makes us steadfast, gives us courage, makes the desert and the steppe rejoice and blossom—that is, when our lives become arid. And when do our lives become arid? When they lack the water of God's Word and his Spirit of love. However great our limitations and dismay, we are not allowed to be sluggish and vacillating when faced with difficulty and our own weakness. On the contrary, we are invited to strengthen the weak hands, to make firm the feeble knees, to be strong and to fear not, because our God always shows us the greatness of his mercy.

He gives us the strength to go forward. He is always with us in order to help us go forward. He is a God who loves us so very much. He loves us and that is why he is with us, to help us, to strengthen us, to help us go forward. Courage! Always forward! Thanks to his help, we can always begin again. How? Begin again from scratch. Someone might say to me, "No, Father, I did so many reprehensible things . . . I am a great sinner . . . I cannot begin from scratch!" You are wrong! You can begin from scratch. Why? Because he is waiting for you, he is close to you, he loves you, he is merciful, he forgives you, he gives you the strength to begin again from scratch! Everybody! And so we are able to open our eyes again, to overcome sadness and mourning to strike up a new song. And this true joy remains even amid trial, even amid suffering, for it is not a superficial joy; it permeates the depths of the person who entrusts himself to the Lord and confides in him.

God is God-with-us, God who loves us, God who walks with us. This is the message of Christmas: the Word became flesh. Thus, Christmas reveals to us the immense love God has for humanity. From this too derives our enthusiasm, our hope as Christians, that in our poverty we may know that we are loved, that we have been visited, that we are accompanied by God. And we look upon the world and on history as a place in which we walk together with him and among us toward a new heaven and a new earth.

And to truly welcome Jesus into our life and to prolong the joy of the Holy Night, the path is the very one indicated in Matthew 10:17–22—that is, to bear witness to Jesus in humility, in silent service, without fear of going against the current and of praying in the first person. And if not all are called, like St. Stephen, to shed their blood, each Christian is, however, asked to be consistent in every circumstance with the faith that he or she professes. And

Christian consistency is a grace that we must ask of the Lord. To be consistent, to live as Christians and not to say, "I am a Christian" but live as a pagan. Consistency is a grace we must ask for today.

The Gospel of Luke 15 contains three parables of mercy: the lost sheep, the lost coin, and then the longest of them, characteristic of St. Luke, the parable of the father of two sons, the "prodigal" son and the son who believes he is "righteous," who believes he is saintly. All three of these parables speak of the joy of God. God is joyful. This is interesting: God is joyful! And what is the joy of God? The joy of God is forgiving. . . . The joy of a shepherd who finds his little lamb; the joy of a woman who finds her coin; it is the joy of a father welcoming home the son who was lost, who was as though dead and has come back to life, who has come home. Here is the entire Gospel—here! The whole Gospel, all of Christianity, is here. But make sure that it is not sentiment, a matter of simply being a "do-gooder." On the contrary, mercy is the true force that can save humanity and the world from the cancer that is sin, moral evil, and spiritual evil. Only love fills . . . the negative chasms that evil opens in hearts and in history. Only love can do this, and this is God's joy.

Jesus is not a lone missionary; he does not want to fulfill his mission alone but involves his disciples. In addition to the twelve apostles he calls another seventy-two and sends them to the villages, two by two, to proclaim that the Kingdom of God is close at hand. This is very beautiful! Jesus does not want to act alone; he came to bring the love of God into the world, and he wants to spread it in the style of communion, in the style of brotherhood. That is why he immediately forms a community of disciples, which is a missionary community. He trains them straight away for the mission, to go forth.

The Gospel of Luke tells us that those seventy-two came back from their mission full of joy because they had experienced the power of Christ's name over evil. Jesus says it: to these disciples he gives the power to defeat the evil one. But he adds, "Do not rejoice in this, that the spirits are subject to you;

but rejoice that your names are written in heaven" (Luke 10:20). We should not boast as if we were the protagonists: there is only one protagonist, the Lord! The Lord's grace is the protagonist. He is the one hero. And our joy is just this: to be his disciples, his friends. May Our Lady help us to be good agents of the Gospel.

The Church stands entirely *within this movement* of God toward the world: her joy is the Gospel, to mirror the light of Christ. The Church is the people who have experienced this attraction and bear it within, in their hearts and in their lives. I would like to say—sincerely—I would like to say to those who feel far from God and from the Church; I would like to say respectively to all those who are

> *The Church stands entirely within this movement of God toward the world: her joy is the Gospel, to mirror the light of Christ.*

fearful or indifferent: "The Lord is also calling you to be a part of his people, and he does so with deep respect and love!" The Lord is calling you. The Lord is seeking you. The Lord is waiting for you. The Lord does not proselytize; he loves, and this love seeks you, waits for you, you who at this moment do not believe or are far away. And this is the love of God.

In Thessalonians 5:17–22 St. Paul indicates the conditions for being "missionaries of joy": praying constantly, always giving thanks to God, giving way to his Spirit, seeking the good and avoiding evil. If this becomes our lifestyle, then the Good News will be able to enter so many homes and help people and families rediscover that in Jesus lies salvation. In him it is possible to find interior peace and the strength to face different life situations every day, even the heaviest and most difficult.

In the Gospel of Luke 24:36–49 the disciples could not believe the joy they felt, because they could not believe the cause of this joy. This is what the Gospel tells us. Let's set the scene: Jesus has risen; the disciples of Emmaus are speaking about their experience, and Peter also is recounting what he had seen. Then the Lord himself appears in the room and says to them, "Peace be with you." Many feelings erupt in the hearts of the disciples: fear, surprise, doubt, and—finally—joy. A joy so great that they "could not believe it." They are shocked and stunned; and Jesus, almost with a faint smile, asks them for something to eat and starts explaining the Scriptures, opening their minds so they are able to understand them. This is the moment of astonishment, of the encounter with Jesus Christ, where so much joy doesn't seem real; even more, to feel joy and happiness in that moment seems risky and we feel tempted to take shelter in skepticism, in "not exaggerating."

It is easier to believe in a ghost than in the living Christ. It is easier to go to a magician who predicts the future, a fortune-teller, than to have faith and hope in a victorious Christ, in a Christ who triumphed over death. It is easier to have an idea, an imagination, than docility to this Lord who rose from the dead than to go and learn what he has in store for one! Such a manner of relativizing the faith ends with distancing oneself from the encounter, with moving away from God's caress. It's as if we "distill" the reality of the encounter with Jesus Christ in a still of fear, in a still of excessive safety, of wishing to control the encounter ourselves. The disciples were afraid of this joy . . . and so are we.

The Acts of the Apostles 3:1–9 speaks of a paralyzed man. We . . . all know about the transformation of this man, crippled from birth, lying at the door to the Temple asking for alms, without ever crossing the threshold, and how his eyes were fixed on the apostles, waiting for them to give him something. Peter and John could give him nothing he asked for: neither gold nor silver. And he, who always waited at the door, now enters on his own two feet, jumping and praising God, praising God's wonders. And his joy is contagious. This is what the Scripture tells us today: the people were completely astonished and amazed, and they flocked to see this wonder. In the midst of that confusion, of that admiration, Peter proclaimed the message. The joy of the encounter with Jesus Christ, which we are so afraid of accepting, is contagious, and he shouts the news: it is here the Church grows! The paralyzed man believes because "the Church does not grow from proselytizing, but from attraction"; this joy's testimony that proclaims Jesus Christ attracts people. This is witness born from the joy accepted and then transformed into proclamation.

We who are baptized, children of the Church, are called to accept ever anew the presence of God among us and to help others discover him, or to rediscover what they have forgotten. It is a most beautiful mission, like that of John the Baptist: to direct the people to Christ—not to ourselves!—for he is the destination to which the human heart tends when it seeks joy and happiness.

Without this joy, without this glee, we cannot found a Church! We cannot establish a Christian community! It is an apostolic joy that radiates and expands. Like Peter, I ask myself, "Am I able, like Peter, to sit next to my brother and slowly explain the gift of the Word that I have received and infect him with my joy? Am I capable of arousing around me the enthusiasm of those who discover in us the miracle of a new life, which cannot be controlled, which demands docility because it draws us, it carries us; and is this new life born from the encounter with Christ?"

We cannot be messengers of God's comfort if we do not first feel the joy of being comforted and loved by him. This happens especially when we hear his Word, the Gospel, which we should carry in our pocket: do not forget this—the Gospel in your pocket or purse, to read regularly. And this gives us comfort: when we abide in silent prayer in his presence, when we encounter him in the Eucharist or in the sacrament of reconciliation. All this comforts us.

The prophet Isaiah (61:1–2) suggests another dimension that will help us experience joy. It is to bring others the Good News: We are Christians. *Christian* comes from *Christ*, and *Christ* means "anointed." And we too are "anointed." . . . *Christians* means "anointed ones." And why are we anointed? To do what? "He sent me to bring the good news" to whom? "To the poor, to bind up the brokenhearted, to proclaim liberty to the captives, and the opening of the prison to those who are bound; to proclaim the year of the Lord's favor" (see Isa. 61:1–2). This is the vocation of Christ and the vocation of Christians as well. To go to others, to those in need, whether their needs be material or spiritual. . . . Many people who suffer anxiety because of family problems . . . To bring peace there, to bring the unction of Jesus, the oil of Jesus, which does so much good and consoles souls.

No one has ever heard of a sad saint with a mournful face. This is unheard of! It would be a contradiction. The Christian's heart is filled with peace because he knows how to place his joy in the Lord even when going through the difficult moments in life. To have faith does not mean to never have difficult moments but to have the strength to face those moments knowing that we are not alone. And this is the peace that God gives to his children.

# 6

# The Presence of God in the Family

---

The image of God is the married couple: the man and the woman—not only the man, not only the woman, but both of them together. This is the image of God: love. God's covenant with us is represented in that covenant between man and woman. And this is very beautiful! We are created in order to love, as a reflection of God and his love. And in the marital union man and woman fulfill this vocation through their mutual reciprocity and their full and definitive communion of life.

When a man and a woman celebrate the sacrament of matrimony, God, as it were, is "mirrored" in them; he impresses in them his own features and the indelible character of his love. Marriage is the icon of God's love for us. Indeed, God is communion too: the three Persons of the Father, the Son, and the Holy Spirit live eternally in perfect unity. And this is precisely the mystery of matrimony: God makes of the two spouses one single life.

The Bible uses a powerful expression and says "one flesh," so intimate is the union between a man and a woman in marriage. And this is precisely the mystery of marriage: the love of God that is reflected in the couple that decides to live together. Therefore, a man leaves his home, the home of his parents, and goes to live with his wife and unites himself so strongly to her that the two become—the Bible says—one flesh.

St. Paul, in the letter to the Ephesians, emphasizes that a great mystery is reflected in Christian spouses: the relationship established by Christ with the Church, a nuptial relationship (see Eph. 5:21–33). The Church is the bride of Christ. This is their relationship. This means that matrimony responds to a specific vocation and must be considered as a consecration (see *Gaudium et spes*, n. 48: *Familiaris consortio*, n. 56). It is a consecration; the man and woman are consecrated in their love. The spouses, in fact, in virtue of the sacrament, are invested with a true and proper mission, so that starting with the simple ordinary things of life they may make visible the love with which Christ loves his Church, by continuing to give his life for her in fidelity and service.

There is a truly marvelous design inherent in the sacrament of matrimony! And it unfolds in the simplicity and frailty of the human condition. We are well aware of how many difficulties two spouses experience. . . . The important thing is to keep alive their bond with God, who stands as the foundation of the marital bond. And the true bond is always the Lord. When the family prays, the bond is preserved. When the husband prays for his wife and the wife prays for her husband, that bond becomes strong; one praying for the other.

There are three [phrases] that always need to be said . . . at home: "May I?" "Thank you," and "Sorry." The three magic [phrases]. *May I*: so as not to be intrusive. May I, but how does it seem to you? May I, please allow me. *Thank you*: to thank one's spouse; thank you for what you did for me, thank you for this. That beauty of giving thanks! And since we all make mistakes, that other word that is a bit hard to say but that needs to be said: *sorry*. *Please*, *thank you*, and *sorry*. With these . . . words, with the prayer of the husband for the wife and vice versa, by always making peace before the day comes to an end, [they will help their] marriage go forward.

Dear families, you know very well that the true joy we experience in the family is not superficial; it does not come from material objects, from the fact that everything seems to be going well. . . . True joy comes from a profound harmony between persons, something we all feel in our hearts and that makes us experience the beauty of togetherness, of mutual support along life's journey. But the basis of this feeling of deep joy is the presence of God, the presence of God in the family, and his love, which is welcoming, merciful, and respectful toward all.

How important grandparents are for family life, for passing on the human and religious heritage so essential for each and every society! How important it is to have intergenerational exchanges and dialogue, especially within the context of the family. The Aparecida Document says, "Children and the elderly build the future of peoples: children because they lead history forward, the elderly because they transmit the experience and wisdom of their lives" (no. 447). This relationship and this dialogue between generations is a treasure to be preserved and strengthened.

*True joy comes from a profound harmony between persons, something we all feel in our hearts and that makes us experience the beauty of togetherness, of mutual support along life's journey.*

And Jesus heals: let yourselves be healed by Jesus. We all have wounds, everyone: spiritual wounds, sins, hostility, jealousy. Perhaps we don't say hello to someone: "Ah, he did this to me. I won't acknowledge him anymore." But this needs to be healed! "How do I do it?" Pray and ask that Jesus heal it. It's sad in a family when siblings don't speak to each other for a small matter, because the devil takes a small matter and makes a world of it. Then hostilities go on, often for many years, and that family is destroyed. Parents suffer because their children don't speak to each other, or one son's wife doesn't speak to the other, and thus, with jealousy, envy. . . . The devil sows this. And the only One who casts out demons is Jesus. The only One who heals these matters is Jesus. For this reason I say to each one of you: let yourself be healed by Jesus.

[W]hat is the power that unites the family? It is indeed love, and the one who sows love in our hearts is God, God's love. It is precisely God's love that gives meaning to our small daily tasks and helps us face the great trials. This is the true treasure of humankind: going forward in life with love, with that love the Lord has sown in our hearts, with God's love. This is the true treasure. But what is God's love? It is not something vague, some generic feeling. God's love has a name and a face: Jesus Christ. Love for God is made manifest in Jesus. For we cannot love air. . . . Do we love air? Do we love all things?

No, no we cannot; we love people, and the person we love is Jesus, the gift of the Father among us.

Each Christian family can first of all—as Mary and Joseph did—welcome Jesus, listen to him, speak with him, guard him, protect him, grow with him, and in this way improve the world. Let us make room in our heart and in our day for the Lord, as Mary and Joseph also did, and it was not easy. How many difficulties they had to overcome! They were not a superficial family, they were not an unreal family. The family of Nazareth urges us to rediscover the vocation and mission of the family, of every family.

[Jesus' love] is a love that gives value and beauty to everything else, a love that gives strength to the family, to work, to study, to friendship, to art, to all human activity. It gives meaning even to negative experiences because this love allows us to move beyond these experiences . . . not to remain prisoners of evil. [This love] moves us beyond, always opening us to hope, that's it! Love of God in Jesus always opens us to hope, to that horizon of hope, to the final horizon of our pilgrimage. In this way our labors and failures find meaning.

All families need God—all of us! We need his help, his strength, his blessing, his mercy, his forgiveness. And we need simplicity to pray as a family; simplicity is necessary! Praying the Our Father together, around the table, is not something extraordinary: it's easy. And praying the rosary together, as a family, is very beautiful and a source of great strength. And also praying for one another—the husband for his wife, the wife for her husband, both together for their children, the children for their grandparents . . . praying for one another. This is what it means to pray in the family, and prayer is what makes the family strong.

We can imagine that the Virgin Mary in Luke 1:39–56, visiting the home of Elizabeth, would have heard her and her husband, Zechariah, praying in the words of Psalm 71: "You, O Lord, are my hope, my trust, O Lord, from my youth. . . . Do not cast me off in the time of old age, do not forsake me when my strength is spent. . . . Even to old age and grey hairs, O God, do not forsake me, until I proclaim your might to all the generations to come." The young Mary listened, and she kept all these things in her heart. The wisdom of Elizabeth and Zechariah enriched her young spirit. They were no experts in parenthood; for them too it was the first pregnancy. But they were experts in faith, experts in God, and experts in the hope that comes from him; and this is what the world needs in every age. Mary was able to listen to those elderly and amazed parents; she treasured their wisdom, and it proved precious for her in her journey as a woman, as a wife, and as a mother.

Before our eyes we can picture Mother Mary as she walks, carrying the baby Jesus in her arms. She brings him to the Temple; she presents him to the people; she brings him to meet his people.

We can imagine this tiny family, in the midst of so many people, in the Temple's grand courtyards. They do not stand out, are not distinguishable. . . . Yet they do not pass unnoticed! Two elderly people, Simeon and Anna, moved by the Holy Spirit, approach and praise God for that Child, in whom they recognize the Messiah, the light of the people and the salvation of Israel (see Luke 2:22–38). It is a simple moment but rich with prophecy: the encounter between two young spouses full of joy and faith due to the grace of the Lord, and two elderly people also filled with joy and faith through the action of the Spirit. Who causes them to meet? Jesus. Jesus brings them together, young and old.

Jesus is he who brings generations closer. He is the font of that love that unites families and people, conquering all diffidence, all isolation, all distance. This causes us to think also of grandparents: how important is the presence of grandparents! How precious their role is in the family and in society. A good relationship between the young and the elderly is crucial for the journey of the civil and ecclesial community. Looking at these two elderly people—Simeon and Anna—let us greet from here, with applause, all the world's grandparents.

The baby Jesus with his mother, Mary, and with St. Joseph becomes a simple but so luminous icon of the family. The light it casts is the light of mercy and salvation for all the world, the light of truth for every person, for the human family and for individual families. This light, which comes from the Holy Family, encourages us to offer human warmth in those family situations in which, for various reasons, peace is lacking, harmony is lacking, and forgiveness is lacking. May our concrete solidarity not diminish, especially with regard to the families who are experiencing more difficult situations. . . . Let us pause here for a moment and pray in silence for all these families in difficulty, whether due to problems of illness, unemployment, discrimination, or need to emigrate, due to difficulty in understanding one another and also to disunion. . . . Let us entrust to Mary, Queen and Mother of the family, all the families of the world, that they may live in faith, in accord, in reciprocal aid, and for this I invoke upon them the maternal protection of the one who was the mother and daughter of her Son.

The Gospel of Matthew tells us how the Holy Family [traveled] on the sorrowful road of exile, seeking refuge in Egypt (2:13–15). Joseph, Mary, and Jesus experienced the tragic fate of refugees, which is marked by fear, uncertainty, and unease. Unfortunately, in our own time, millions of families can identify with this sad reality. Almost every day the television and papers carry news of refugees fleeing from hunger, war, and other grave dangers, in search of security and a dignified life for themselves and for their families.

In distant lands, even when they find work, refugees and immigrants do not always find a true welcome, respect, and appreciation for the values they bring. Their legitimate expectations collide with complex and difficult situations that at times seem insurmountable. Therefore, as we fix our gaze on the Holy Family of Nazareth as they were forced to become refugees, let us think of the tragedy of those migrants and refugees who are victims of rejection and exploitation, who are victims of human trafficking and of slave labor. But let us also think of the other "exiles": I would call them "hidden exiles," those exiles who can be found within their own families: the elderly, for example, who are sometimes treated as a burdensome presence. I often think that a good indicator for knowing how a family is doing is seeing how their children and elderly are treated.

Jesus wanted to belong to a family who experienced these hardships, so that no one would feel excluded from the loving closeness of God. The flight into Egypt caused by Herod's threat shows us that God is present where we are in danger, where we are suffering, where we are fleeing, where we experience rejection and abandonment. But God is also present where we dream, where we hope to return in freedom to our homeland and plan and choose life for our families and dignity for ourselves and our loved ones.

Jesus dwelt on [the] periphery for thirty years. The evangelist Luke summarizes this period like this: Jesus "was obedient to them"—that is, to Mary and Joseph. And someone might say, "But did this God, who comes to save us, waste thirty years there, in that suburban slum?" He wasted thirty years! He wanted this. Jesus' path was in that family: "and his mother kept all these things in her heart. And Jesus increased in wisdom and in stature, and in favor with God and man" (Luke 2:51–52). [Scripture] does not recount miracles or healing, or preaching—Jesus did none in that period—or of crowds flocking. In Nazareth everything seemed to happen "normally" according to the customs of a pious and hardworking Israelite family: they worked, the mother cooked, she did all the housework . . . all the things mothers do. The father, a carpenter, worked, taught his son the trade. Thirty years. "But what a waste, Father!" God works in mysterious ways. But what was important is that there was the family! And this was not a waste! They were great saints: Mary, the most holy woman, immaculate, and Joseph, a most righteous man. . . . The family.

We are certainly moved by the story of how the adolescent Jesus followed the religious calendar of the community and the social duties; in knowing how, as a young worker, he worked with Joseph; and then how he attended the reading of the Scriptures, in praying the psalms and in so many other customs of daily life. The Gospels, in their sobriety, make no reference to Jesus' adolescence and leave this task to our loving meditation. Art, literature, and music have taken this journey through imagination. It is certainly not difficult to imagine how much mothers could learn from Mary's care for that son! And how much fathers could glean from the example of Joseph, a righteous man, who dedicated his life to supporting and protecting the child and his wife—his family—in difficult times. Not to mention how much children could be encouraged by the adolescent Jesus to understand the necessity and beauty of cultivating their most profound vocation and of dreaming great dreams! In those thirty years, Jesus cultivated his vocation for which the

Father had sent him. And in that time, Jesus never became discouraged but increased in courage in order to carry his mission forward.

What happened in those thirty years in Nazareth can thus happen to us too: we can seek to make love, not hate, normal, making mutual help, not indifference or enmity, commonplace. It is no coincidence, then, that *Nazareth* means "she who keeps," as Mary "kept all these things in her heart." Since then, each time there is a family that keeps this mystery, even if it is on the periphery of the world, the mystery of the Son of God, the mystery of Jesus who comes to save us, the mystery is at work. He comes to save the world. And this is the great mission of the family: to make room for Jesus who is coming, to welcome Jesus in the family, in each member: children, husband, wife, grandparents. . . . Jesus is there. Welcome him there, in order that he grow spiritually in the family.

We hear the same message in the apostle Paul's exhortation to Timothy and, through him, to the Christian community. Jesus did not abolish the law of the family and the passing of generations but brought it to fulfillment. The Lord formed a new family in which bonds of kinship are less important than our relationship with him and our doing the will of God the Father. Yet the love of Jesus and the Father completes and fulfills our love for parents, brothers and sisters, and grandparents; it renews family relationships with the lymph of the Gospel and of the Holy Spirit.

St. Paul urges Timothy, who was a pastor and hence a father to the community, to show respect for the elderly and other members of the family. He tells him to do so like a son: treating "older men as fathers," "older women as mothers," and "younger women as sisters." The head of the community is not exempt from following the will of God in this way; indeed, the love of Christ impels him to do so with an even greater love. Like the Virgin Mary, who, though she became the mother of the Messiah, felt herself driven by the love of God taking flesh within her to hasten to her elderly relative Elizabeth.

Today our gaze on the Holy Family lets us also be drawn into the simplicity of the life they led in Nazareth. It is an example that does our families great good, helping them increasingly to become communities of love and reconciliation, in which tenderness, mutual help, and mutual forgiveness are experienced. Let us remember the three key phrases for living in peace and joy in the family: "May I?" "Thank you," and "Sorry." In our family, when we are not intrusive and ask, "May I?"; in our family, when we are not selfish and learn to say, "Thank you"; and when in a family one realizes he has done something wrong and knows how to say, "I'm sorry"—in such a family there are peace and joy. Let us remember these important phrases. . . . I would also like to encourage families to become aware of the importance they have in the Church and in society. The proclamation of the Gospel, in fact, first passes through the family to reach the various spheres of daily life.

Let us fervently call upon Mary Most Holy, the Mother of Jesus and our Mother, and St. Joseph her spouse. Let us ask them to enlighten, comfort, and guide every family in the world, so that they may fulfill with dignity and peace the mission God has entrusted to them.

# 7

# Love Is the Measurement of Faith

In Matthew 22:15–21 Jesus reminds us that the whole of divine law can be summed up in our love for God and neighbor. Matthew the Evangelist recounts that several Pharisees colluded to put Jesus to the test. One of them, a doctor of the law, asked him this question: "Teacher, which is the greatest commandment in the law?" Jesus, quoting the book of Deuteronomy, answered, "You shall love the Lord your God with all your heart, and with all your soul, and with all your mind. This is the greatest and first commandment." And he could have stopped there. Yet, Jesus adds something that was not asked by the doctor of the law. He says, in fact: "And a second is like it, You shall love your neighbor as yourself." And in this case, too, Jesus does not invent the second commandment but takes it from the book of Leviticus. The novelty is in his placing these two commandments together—love for God and love for neighbor—revealing that they are in fact inseparable and complementary, two sides of the same coin. You cannot love God without loving your neighbor, and you cannot love your neighbor without loving God.

In effect, the visible sign a Christian can show to witness to his love for God to the world and to others, to his family, is the love he bears for his brothers. The commandment to love God and neighbor is the first, not because it is at the top of the list of commandments. Jesus does not place it at the pinnacle but at the center, because it is from the heart that everything must go out and to which everything must return and refer.

In Exodus 22:22–26 we see that the requirement to be holy, in the image of God who is holy, included the duty to care for the most vulnerable people, such as the stranger and the orphan. And this covenant law is brought to fulfillment by Jesus—he who unites in himself, in his flesh, divinity and humanity, a single mystery of love.

Now, in the light of this Word of Jesus, love is the measure of faith, and faith is the soul of love. We can no longer separate a religious life, a pious life, from service to brothers and sisters, to the real brothers and sisters we encounter. We can no longer divide prayer, the encounter with God in the sacraments, from listening to the other, closeness to his life, especially to his wounds. Remember this: love is the measure of faith. How much do you love? How is your faith? My faith is as I love. And faith is the soul of love.

In the middle of the dense forest of rules and regulations—the legalisms of past and present—Jesus makes an opening through which one can catch a glimpse of two faces: the face of the Father and the face of the brother. Jesus does not give us two formulas or two precepts; there are no precepts or formulas. He gives us two faces, actually only one real face, that of God reflected in many faces, because in the face of each brother, especially of the smallest, the most fragile, the defenseless and needy, there is God's own image. And we must ask ourselves, When we meet one of these brothers, are we able to recognize the face of God in him? Are we able to do this?

The prophet Isaiah presents [Divine Providence] as the image of maternal love full of tenderness, and thus says: "Can a woman forget her suckling child, that she should have no compassion on the son of her womb? Even these may forget, yet I will not forget you" (Isaiah 49:15). How beautiful is this! God does not forget us, not one of us! Everyone by name and surname. He loves us and doesn't forget. What a beautiful thought. . . . This invitation to trust in God finds a parallel in Matthew 6:26–29: "Look at the birds of the air," Jesus says, "they neither sow nor reap nor gather into barns, and yet your heavenly Father feeds them. . . . Consider the lilies of the field, how they grow: they neither toil nor spin; yet I tell you, even Solomon in all his glory was not arrayed like one of these."

However, thinking of the many people who live in precarious conditions or even in a poverty offensive to their dignity, these words of Jesus could seem abstract, if not illusory. But actually they are relevant, now more than ever! They remind us that you cannot serve two masters: God and wealth. As long as everyone seeks to accumulate for themselves, there will never be justice. We must take heed of this! Instead, by entrusting ourselves to God's providence, and seeking his kingdom together, no one will lack the necessary means to live with dignity.

God's providence comes through our service to others, our sharing with others. If each of us accumulates not for ourselves alone but for the service of others—in this case, in this act of solidarity—the providence of God is made visible. If, however, one accumulates only for oneself, what will happen when one is called by God? No one can take his riches with him, because, as you know, the shroud has no pockets! It is better to share, for we can take with us to heaven only what we have shared with others.

A heart troubled by the desire for possessions is a heart full of desire for possessions but empty of God. That is why Jesus frequently warned the rich, because they greatly risk placing their security in the goods of this world, and security, the final security, is in God. In a heart possessed by wealth there isn't much room for faith; everything is involved with wealth, and there is no room for faith. If, however, one gives God his rightful place—that is, first place—then his love leads one to share even one's wealth, to set it at the service of projects of solidarity and development, as is demonstrated by so many examples, even recent ones, in the history of the Church.

The road Jesus points out can seem a little unrealistic with respect to the common mind-set and to problems due to the economic crisis. But if we think about it, this road leads us back to the right scale of values. In Matthew 6:25 he tells us, "Is not life more than food, and the body more than clothing?" To ensure that no one lacks bread, water, clothing, a home, work, and health, we need to recognize that all people are children of the

Father who is in heaven and, therefore, brothers among us, and that we must act accordingly.

The Gospel of Matthew 4:1–11 sets before us the narrative of the temptation of Jesus, when the Holy Spirit, having descended upon him after his baptism in the Jordan, prompts him to confront Satan openly in the desert for forty days, before beginning his public ministry.

The tempter seeks to divert Jesus from the Father's plan—that is, from the way of sacrifice, of the love that offers itself in expiation—to make him take an easier path, one of success and power. The duel between Jesus and Satan takes place through strong quotations from sacred Scripture. In fact, to divert Jesus from the way of the cross, the devil sets before him false messianic hopes: economic well-being, indicated by the ability to turn stones into bread; a dramatic and miraculous style, with the idea of throwing himself down from the highest point of the Temple in Jerusalem and being saved by angels; and lastly, a shortcut to power and dominion, in exchange for an act of adoration to Satan. These are the three groups of temptations, and we, too, know them well!

Jesus decisively rejects all these temptations and reiterates his firm resolve to follow the path set by the Father, without any kind of compromise with sin or worldly logic. Note well how Jesus responds. He does not dialogue with Satan, as Eve had done in the earthly paradise. Jesus is well aware that there can be no dialogue with Satan, because he is cunning. That is why Jesus, instead of engaging in dialogue as Eve had, chooses to take refuge in the Word of God and responds with the power of this Word.

Let us remember this: at the moment of temptation, of our own temptations, there is no arguing with Satan; our defense must always be the Word of God! And this will save us. In his replies to Satan, the Lord, using the Word of God, reminds us above all that "man shall not live by bread alone, but by every word that proceeds from the mouth of God" (Matt. 4:4); and this gives us the strength, sustains us in the struggle against a worldly mind-set that would lower us to the level of our primitive needs, causing us to lose hunger for what is true, good, and beautiful, the hunger for God and for his love. Furthermore, Jesus recalls that "it is written, 'You shall not tempt the Lord your God,'" for the way of faith passes also through darkness and doubt and is nourished by patience and persevering expectation. Lastly, Jesus recalls that "it is written, 'You shall worship the Lord your God and him only you shall serve.'" [In other words], we must rid ourselves of idols, of vain things, and build our lives on what is essential.

The Bible tells us that the great threat to God's plan for us is, and always has been, the lie. The devil is the father of lies. Often he hides his snares behind the appearance of sophistication, the allure of being "modern," "like everyone else." He distracts us with the view of ephemeral pleasures, superficial pastimes. And so we squander our God-given gifts by tinkering with gadgets; we squander our money on gambling and drink; we turn in on ourselves. We forget to remain focused on the things that really matter. We forget to remain, at heart, children of God. That is sin: forgetting that, at heart, we are children of God. For children, as the Lord tells us, have their own wisdom, which is not the wisdom of the world. That is why the message of the Santo Niño is so important. He speaks powerfully to all of us. He reminds us of our deepest identity, of what we are called to be as God's family.

The poor are at the center of the Gospel, are at heart of the Gospel. If we take away the poor from the Gospel, then we can't understand the whole message of Jesus Christ. As ambassadors for Christ, we—bishops, priests, and religious, [and laity]—ought to be the first to welcome his reconciling grace into our hearts. St. Paul makes clear what this means. It means rejecting worldly perspectives and seeing all things anew in the light of Christ. It means being the first to examine our consciences, to acknowledge our failings and sins, and to embrace the path of constant conversion, every-day conversion. How can we proclaim the newness and liberating power of the cross to others if we ourselves refuse to allow the Word of God to shake our complacency, our fear of change, our petty compromises with the ways of this world, our "spiritual worldliness"?

In Matthew's Gospel we find Jesus' invitation: "Come to me, all who labor and are heavy laden, and I will give you rest" (11:28). When Jesus says this, he has before him the people he meets every day on the streets of Galilee: very many simple people, those who are poor or sick, sinners, those who are marginalized. . . . These people always followed him to hear his word—a word that gave hope! Jesus' words always give hope!—and even just to touch the hem of his garment. Jesus himself sought out these tired, worn-out crowds who were like sheep without a shepherd (see Matt. 9:35–36), and he sought them out to proclaim to them the Kingdom of God and to heal many of them in body and spirit. Now he calls them all to himself: "Come to me," and he promises them relief and rest.

This invitation of Jesus reaches to our day and extends to the many brothers and sisters oppressed by life's precarious conditions, by existential and difficult situations, and at times lacking valid points of reference. In the poorest countries, but also on the outskirts of the richest countries, there are so many weary people, worn out under the unbearable weight of neglect and indifference.

Indifference: human indifference causes the needy so much pain! And worse is the indifference of Christians! On the fringes of society so many men and women are tried by indigence, but also by frustration and by dissatisfaction with life. So many are forced to emigrate from their homeland, risking their lives. Many more, every day, carry the weight of an economic system that exploits human beings, imposing on them an unbearable yoke that the few privileged do not want to bear. To each of these children of the Father in heaven, Jesus repeats: "Come to me, all of you." But he also says it to those who have everything but whose hearts are empty and without God. Even to them, Jesus addresses this invitation: "Come to me." Jesus' invitation is for everyone, but especially for those who suffer the most.

Jesus promises to give rest to everyone, but he also gives us an invitation, which is like a commandment: "Take my yoke upon you, and learn from me; for I am gentle and lowly in heart" (Matt. 11:29). The "yoke" of the

Lord consists in taking on, with fraternal love, the burden of others. Once we receive Christ's comfort and rest, we are called in turn to become rest and comfort for our brothers and sisters, with a docile and humble attitude, in imitation of the Teacher. Docility and humility of heart help us not only to take on the burden of others, but also to keep our personal views, our judgments, our criticism, or our indifference from weighing on them.

From this event we can understand three messages. The first is *compassion*. In facing the crowd who follows him and, so to speak, won't leave him alone, Jesus does not react with irritation; he does not say, "These people are bothering me." No, no. He reacts with a feeling of compassion, because he knows they are not seeking him out of curiosity but out of need. But please note: compassion—which Jesus feels—is

> The "yoke" of the Lord consists in taking on, with fraternal love, the burden of others. Once we receive Christ's comfort and rest, we are called in turn to become rest and comfort for our brothers and sisters.

not simply feeling pity; it's more! It means to *suffer with*, in other words, to empathize with the suffering of another, to the point of taking it upon oneself.

Jesus is like this: he suffers together with us—he suffers with us and suffers for us. And the sign of this compassion is the healing he performed for countless people. Jesus teaches us to place the needs of the poor before our own. Our needs, even if legitimate, are not as urgent as those . . . who lack the basic necessities of life. We often speak of "the poor." But when we speak of them, do we sense that this man or that woman or those children lack the bare necessities of life? That they have no food, no clothing, that they cannot afford medicine? . . . Also that the children do not have the means to attend school? Whereas our needs, although legitimate, are not as urgent as those who lack life's basic necessities.

The second message is *sharing*. The first is compassion, which Jesus felt, and the second is sharing. It's helpful to compare the disciples' reaction to the tired and hungry people with that of Jesus. They are different. The disciples think it would be better to send the people away so they can go and buy food. Jesus says, "You give them something to eat." Two different reactions, which reflect two contrasting outlooks: the disciples reason with worldly logic, by which each person must think of himself; they reason as if to say, "Sort it out for yourselves." Jesus reasons with God's logic, which is that of sharing.

How many times we turn away so as not to see our brothers in need! And this looking away is a polite way to say, "Sort it out for yourselves." And this is not Jesus' way: this is selfishness. Had he sent away the crowds, many people would have been left with nothing to eat. Instead those few loaves and fish, shared and blessed by God, were enough for everyone. And pay heed! It isn't magic but a sign—a sign that calls for faith in God, provident Father, who does not let us go without "our daily bread" if we know how to share it as brothers.

So many men and women of faith have faith but then divide the tablets of the laws. "Yes, I do this." "But do you practice charity?" "Yes of course, I always send a check to the Church." "Okay, that's good. But at your home, within your own church, are you generous and are you fair with those who are your dependents—be they your children, your grandparents, your employees?" You cannot make offerings to the Church on the shoulders of the injustice that you practice toward your dependents. This is a very serious sin: using God as a cover for injustice.

*Compassion, sharing.* And the third message: the miracle of the loaves foreshadows the Eucharist. It is seen in the gesture of Jesus who, before breaking and distributing the loaves, "blessed" them (Matt. 14:19). It is the same gesture Jesus was to make at the Last Supper, when he established the perpetual memorial of his redeeming sacrifice. In the Eucharist Jesus does not give just any bread, but *the* bread of eternal life; he gives himself, offering himself to the Father out of love for us. But we must go to the Eucharist with those sentiments of Jesus, which are compassion and the will to share. One who goes to the Eucharist without having compassion for the needy and without sharing, is not at ease with Jesus.

# 8

# Jesus Has Shared Our Journey

---

The biblical and Christian vision of time and history is not cyclical but linear: it is a journey that moves toward completion. A year that has passed, then, does not lead us to a reality that ends but to a reality that is being fulfilled. It is a further step toward the destination that awaits us: a destination of hope and a destination of happiness, for we shall encounter God, who is the reason for our hope and the source of our happiness.

*Walking*—this verb makes us reflect on the course of history, that long journey that is the history of salvation, starting with Abraham, our father in faith, whom the Lord called one day to set out, to go forth from his country toward the land God would show him. From that time on, our identity as believers has been that of a people making its pilgrim way toward the Promised Land. This history has always been accompanied by the Lord! He is ever faithful to his covenant and to his promises. Because he is faithful, "God is light, and in him there is no darkness at all" (1 John 1:5). Yet on the part of the people there are times of both light and darkness, fidelity and infidelity, obedience and rebellion, times of being a pilgrim people and times of being a people adrift.

[Jesus] has entered our history; he has shared our journey. He came to free us from darkness and to grant us light. In him was revealed the grace, the mercy, and the tender love of the Father: Jesus is Love incarnate. He is not simply a teacher of wisdom; he is not an ideal for which we strive while knowing that we are hopelessly distant from it. He is the meaning of life and history, who has pitched his tent in our midst.

The Gospel account of the Magi (Matt. 2:1–12) describes their journey from the East as a journey of the spirit, as a journey toward the encounter with Christ. They are attentive to signs that indicate his presence; they are tireless in facing the trials of the search; they are courageous in deducing the implications for life that derive from encounter with the Lord. This is life: Christian life is a journey, but one of being attentive, tireless, and courageous. A Christian journeys like this—journeys attentively, tirelessly, courageously. The experience of the Magi evokes the journey of every man and woman toward Christ. As for the Magi, so for us, to seek God means to *journey*—and as I said, attentive, tireless, and courageous—focused on the sky and discerning in the visible sign of the star the invisible God who speaks to our hearts.

The star that is able to lead every person to Jesus is the *Word of God*, the Word that is in the Bible, in the Gospels. The Word of God is the light that guides our journey, nourishes our faith, and regenerates it. It is the Word of God that continually renews our hearts and our communities. Therefore, let us not forget to read it and meditate upon it every day, so that it may become for each like a flame that we bear inside us to illuminate our steps as well as the steps of others who journey beside us, who are perhaps struggling to find the path to Christ. Always with the Word of God! The Word of God carried in your hand: a little Gospel in your pocket, purse, always to be read. Do not forget this: always with me, the Word of God!

When one looks to Christ, one does not err. The Gospel of Luke recounts how Jesus, having returned to Nazareth, where he grew up, entered the synagogue and read, making reference to himself, the passage from the prophet Isaiah where it is written: "The Spirit of the Lord is upon me, because he has anointed me to bring good news to the poor. He has sent me to proclaim release to the captives and recovery of sight to the blind, to set at liberty those who are oppressed, to proclaim the acceptable year of the Lord's favor" (Isa. 4:18–19). Behold how Christ used his humanity—for he also was a man—to proclaim and fulfill the divine plan of redemption and salvation, because he was God; so too must it be for the Church. Through her visible reality, all that can be seen, the sacraments and witness of all us Christians, the Church is called every day to be close to every person, to begin with the one who is poor, the one who suffers, and the one who is marginalized, in such a way as to make all people feel the compassionate and merciful gaze of Jesus.

The apostle tells us that with the resurrection of Jesus something absolutely new happens: we are set free from the slavery of sin and become children of God. That is, we are born to new life. When is this accomplished for us? In the sacrament of baptism. In ancient times, it was customarily received through immersion. The person who was to be baptized walked down into the great basin of the baptistry, stepping out of his clothes, and the bishop or priest poured water on his head three times, baptizing him in the name of the Father, and of the Son, and of the Holy Spirit. Then the baptized person emerged from the basin and put on a new robe, the white one. In other words, by immersing himself in the death and resurrection of Christ he was born to new life. He had become a son of God. In his letter to the Romans, St. Paul wrote: "You have received the spirit of sonship. When we cry 'Abba! Father!' it is the Spirit himself bearing witness with our spirit that we are children of God" (Rom. 8:15–16).

Remain steadfast in the journey of faith, with firm hope in the Lord. This is the secret of our journey! He gives us the courage to swim against the tide. Pay attention[;] . . . this is good for the heart, but we need courage to swim against the tide. Jesus gives us this courage! There are no difficulties, trials, or misunderstandings to fear,

> *Remain steadfast in the journey of faith, with firm hope in the Lord. This is the secret of our journey! He gives us the courage to swim against the tide.*

provided we remain united to God as branches to the vine, provided we do not lose our friendship with him, provided we make ever more room for him in our lives. This is especially so whenever we feel poor, weak, and sinful, because God grants strength to our weakness, riches to our poverty, conversion and forgiveness to our sinfulness. The Lord is so rich in mercy: every time, if we go to him, he forgives us. Let us trust in God's work! With him we can do great things; he will give us the joy of being his disciples, his witnesses. Commit yourselves to great ideals, to the most important things. We Christians were not chosen by the Lord for little things; push onward toward the highest principles.

Always remember this: life is a journey. It is a path, a journey to meet Jesus—at the end, and forever. A journey in which we do not encounter Jesus is not a Christian journey. It is for the Christian to continually encounter Jesus, to watch him, to let himself be watched over by Jesus, because Jesus watches us with love. He loves us so much, and he is always watching over us. To encounter Jesus also means allowing oneself to be gazed upon by him. "But, Father, you know," one of you might say to me, "you know that this journey is horrible for me. I am such a sinner, I have committed many sins . . . how can I encounter Jesus?" And you know that the people whom Jesus most sought out were the greatest sinners, and they reproached him for this. And the people—those who believed themselves righteous—would say: this is no true prophet; look what lovely company he keeps! He was with sinners. . . . And he said: I came for those in need of salvation, in need of healing. Jesus heals our sins. And along the way Jesus comes and forgives us—all of us sinners, we are all sinners—even when we make a mistake, when we commit a sin. . . . And this forgiveness that we receive in confession is an encounter with Jesus. We always encounter Jesus.

At the beginning of Mass, every time, we are called before the Lord to recognize that we are sinners, expressing through words and gestures sincere repentance of the heart. And we say, "Have mercy on me, Lord. I am a sinner! I confess to Almighty God my sins." And we don't say, "Lord, have mercy on this man who is beside me, or this woman, who are sinners." No! "Have mercy on me!" We are all sinners and in need of the Lord's forgiveness. It is the Holy Spirit who speaks to our spirit and makes us recognize our faults in light of the Word of Jesus. And Jesus himself invites us all, saints and sinners, to his table, gathering us from the crossroads, from diverse situations of life (see Matt. 22:9–10). And among the conditions in common among those participating in the Eucharistic celebration, two are fundamental in order to go to Mass correctly: we are all sinners, and God grants his mercy to all. These are the two conditions that open wide the doors that we might enter Mass properly.

The road to Emmaus [is] a symbol of our journey of faith: the Scriptures and the Eucharist are the indispensable elements for encountering the Lord.

We too often go to Sunday Mass with our worries, difficulties, and disappointments. . . . Life sometimes wounds us and we go away feeling sad, toward our "Emmaus," turning our backs on God's plan. We distance ourselves from God. But the Liturgy of the Word welcomes us: Jesus explains the Scriptures to us and rekindles in our hearts the warmth of faith and hope, and in communion he gives us strength. The Word of God, the Eucharist. Read a passage of the Gospel every day. Remember it well. Read a passage from the Gospel every day, and on Sundays go to communion, to receive Jesus. This is what happened to the disciples of Emmaus: they received the Word; they shared the breaking of bread; and from feeling sad and defeated they became joyful. Dear brothers and sisters, the Word of God and the Eucharist fill us with joy always. Remember it well! When you are sad, take up the Word of God. When you are down, take up the Word of God and go to Sunday Mass and receive communion, to participate in the mystery of Jesus. The Word of God, the Eucharist: they fill us with joy.

We know that this increasingly artificial world would have us live in a culture of "doing," of the "useful," where we exclude God from our horizon without realizing it. But we also exclude the horizon itself! Lent beacons us to "rouse ourselves," to remind ourselves that we are creatures—simply put, that we are not God. In the little daily scene, as I look at some of the power struggles to occupy spaces, I think, *These people are playing God the Creator. They still have not realized that they are not God.*

In our personal history, too, there are both bright and dark moments, lights and shadows. If we love God and our brothers and sisters, we walk in the light; but if our heart is closed, if we are dominated by pride, deceit, and self-seeking, then darkness falls within us and around us. "Whoever hates his brother," writes the apostle John, "is in the darkness; he walks in the darkness, and does not know the way to go, because the darkness has blinded his eyes" (1 John 2:11). A people who walk, but as a pilgrim people who do not want to go astray.

Only when the difficulties and suffering of others confront and question us may we begin our journey of conversion toward Easter. It is an itinerary that involves the cross and self-denial. Today's Gospel indicates the elements of this spiritual journey: prayer, fasting, and almsgiving. All three exclude the need for appearances. What counts is not appearances; the value of life does not depend on the approval of others or on success, but on what we have inside us.

The first element is prayer. Prayer is the strength of the Christian and of every person who believes. In the weakness and frailty of our lives, we can turn to God with the confidence of children and enter into communion with him. In the face of so many that hurt us and could harden our hearts, we are called to dive into the sea of prayer, which is the sea of God's boundless love, to taste his tenderness. Lent is a time of prayer, of more intense prayer, more prolonged, more assiduous, and more able to take on the needs of the brethren—intercessory prayer, to intercede before God for the many situations of poverty and suffering.

The second key element of the Lenten journey is fasting. We must be careful not to practice a formal fast or one that in truth "satisfies" us because it makes us feel good about ourselves. Fasting makes sense if it questions our security and if it also leads to some benefit for others, if it helps us cultivate the style of the Good Samaritan, who bends down to his brother in need and takes care of him. Fasting involves choosing a sober lifestyle, a way of life that does not waste, a way of life that does not "throw away." Fasting helps us attune our hearts to the essential and to sharing. It is a sign of awareness and responsibility in the face of injustice and abuse, especially to the poor and the little ones, and it is a sign of the trust we place in God and in his providence.

The third element is almsgiving: it points to giving freely, for in almsgiving one gives something to someone from whom one does not expect to receive anything in return. Gratuitousness should be one of the characteristics of the Christian, who, aware of having received everything from God gratuitously—that is, without any merit of his own—learns to give freely to others. Today gratuitousness is often not part of daily life, in which everything is bought and sold. Everything is calculated and measured. Almsgiving helps us experience giving freely, which leads to freedom from the obsession of possessing, from the fear of losing what we have, from the sadness of one who does not wish to share his wealth with others.

God invites us to pray insistently not because he is unaware of our needs or because he is not listening to us. On the contrary, he is always listening and he knows everything about us lovingly. On our daily journey, especially in times of difficulty, in the battle against the evil that is outside and within us, the Lord is not far away, he is by our side. We battle with him beside us, and our weapon is prayer, which makes us feel his presence beside us, his mercy, and also his help. But the battle against evil is a long and hard one; it requires patience and endurance, as when Moses had to keep his arms outstretched for the people to prevail (Exod. 17:8–13). This is how it is: there is a battle to be waged each day, but God is our ally, faith in him is our strength, and prayer is the expression of this faith. Therefore, Jesus assures us of the victory, but at the end he asks, "When the Son of man comes, will he find faith on earth?" (Luke 18:8). If faith is snuffed out, prayer is snuffed out, and we walk in the dark. We become lost on the path of life.

We, the disciples of Jesus, are called to be people who listen to his voice and take his words seriously. To listen to Jesus, we must be close to him, follow him, like the crowd in the Gospel who chased him through the streets of Palestine. Jesus did not have a teaching post or a fixed pulpit; he was an itinerant teacher, who proposed his teachings, teachings given to him by the Father, along the streets, covering distances that were not always predictable or easy. [Now as then, people have to follow] Jesus in order to listen to him.

But also let us listen to Jesus in his written Word, in the Gospel. I pose a question to you: do you read a passage of the Gospel every day? Yes, no . . . yes, no . . . half of the time . . . some yes, some no. It is important! Do you read the Gospel? It is so good; it is a good thing to have a small book of the Gospel, a little one, and to carry . . . and read a short passage in whatever moment presents itself during the day. In any given moment of the day, I take the Gospel from my pocket and I read something, a short passage. Jesus is there and he speaks to us in the Gospel! Ponder this. It's not difficult, nor is it necessary to have all four books; [we can carry] one of the Gospels, a small one, with us. Let the Gospel be with us always, because it is the Word of Jesus in order for us to be able to listen to him.

Read the Gospel. Read the Gospel. . . . Carry a little Gospel with us, . . . in some way, to keep it at hand. And there, reading a passage, we will find Jesus. Everything takes on meaning when you find your treasure there, in the Gospel. Jesus calls it "the Kingdom of God," that is to say, God who reigns in your life, in our life—God who is love, peace, and joy in every man and in all men. This is what God wants, and it is why Jesus gave himself up to death on the cross, to free us from the power of darkness and to move us to the kingdom of life, of beauty, of goodness, and of joy. To read the Gospel is to find Jesus and to have this Christian joy, which is a gift of the Holy Spirit.

In addition, attending Sunday Mass, where we encounter the Lord in the community, we hear his Word and receive the Eucharist, which unites us with him and to one another. And then days of retreat and spiritual exercises are very important for spiritual renewal. Gospel, Eucharist, prayer. Do not forget: Gospel, Eucharist, prayer. Thanks to these gifts of the Lord we are able to conform not to the world but to Christ, and to follow him on his path, the path of "losing one's life" in order to find it (Matt. 16:25). "To lose it" in the sense of giving it, offering it through love and in love—and this leads to sacrifice, also the cross—to receive it, liberated from selfishness and from the mortgage of death, newly purified, full of eternity.

# 9

# The Holy Spirit Is the Soul of Mission

The older theologians used to say that the soul is a kind of sailboat, the Holy Spirit is the wind that fills its sails and drives it forward, and the gusts of wind are the gifts of the Spirit. Lacking his impulse and his grace, we do not go forward. The Holy Spirit draws us into the mystery of the living God and saves us from the threat of a Church that is gnostic and self-referential, closed in on herself. He impels us to open the doors and go forth to proclaim and bear witness to the good news of the Gospel, to communicate the joy of faith, the encounter with Christ.

Speaking to the apostles at the Last Supper, Jesus said that after he left this world he would send them *the gift of the Father*, that is, the Holy Spirit (see John 15:26). This promise was powerfully fulfilled on the day of Pentecost, when the Holy Spirit descended upon the disciples, who were gathered in the Upper Room. This extraordinary outpouring was not limited solely to that moment but was an event that was renewed and still continues to be renewed.

A fundamental element of Pentecost is *astonishment*. Our God is a God of *astonishment*; this we know. No one expected anything more from the disciples: after Jesus' death they were a small, insignificant group of defeated orphans of their master. There occurred instead an unexpected event that astounded: the people were astonished because each of them heard the disciples speaking in their own tongues, telling of the great works of God (see Acts 2:6–7, 11). The Church born at Pentecost is an astounding community because, with the force of her arrival from God, a new message is proclaimed—the resurrection of Christ—with a new language, the universal one of love. A new proclamation: Christ lives; he is risen. A new language: the language of love. The disciples are adorned with power from above and speak with courage. Only minutes before, they all were cowardly, but now they speak with courage and candor, with the freedom of the Holy Spirit.

The Holy Spirit, who has wholly animated the life and mystery of Jesus, is the same Spirit who today guides Christian existence, the existence of men and women who call themselves Christians and want to be Christians. To subject our Christian life and mission, which we have all received in baptism, to the action of the Holy Spirit means that we find the apostolic courage necessary to overcome easy worldly accommodations. Christians and communities who are instead "deaf" to the voice of the Holy Spirit, who urges us to bring the Gospel to the ends of the earth and of society, also become "mutes" who do not speak and do not evangelize.

But who is the Holy Spirit? In the Creed we profess with faith: "I believe in the Holy Spirit, the Lord and Giver of life." The first truth to which we adhere in the Creed is that the Holy Spirit is *Kýrios*, Lord. This signifies that he is truly God, as are the Father and the Son. [The Holy Spirit is, to us,] the object of the same act of adoration and glorification that we address to the Father and to the Son. Indeed, the Holy Spirit is the third person of the Most Holy Trinity; he is the great gift of Christ risen who opens our mind and our hearts to faith in Jesus as the Son sent by the Father and who leads us to friendship, to communion with God.

*The Holy Spirit, who has wholly animated the life and mystery of Jesus, is the same Spirit who today guides Christian existence, the existence of men and women who call themselves Christians and want to be Christians.*

The day of Pentecost, when the disciples "were all filled with the Holy Spirit," was the baptism of the Church, which was born in "going out," in departure to proclaim the Good News to everyone. The Mother Church departs in order to serve. Let us remember the other Mother, our Mother who sets out in haste to serve. Mother Church and Mother Mary: both virgins, both mothers, both women. Jesus was peremptory with the apostles: do not depart from Jerusalem, but wait until you have received the power of the Holy Spirit from above (see Acts 1:4–8). Without him there is no mission, there is no evangelization. For this, with the whole Church, with our Mother Catholic Church, let us implore, "Come, Holy Spirit!"

We turn to the Virgin Mary, who in that Pentecost morning was in the Upper Room, the Mother with her children. In her, the force of the Holy Spirit truly accomplished "great things" (Luke 1:49). She herself said so. May she, the Mother of the Redeemer and Mother of the Church, obtain through her intercession a renewed outpouring of God's Spirit upon the Church and upon the world.

I would like to focus especially on the fact that *the Holy Spirit is the inexhaustible source of God's life in us.* A person of every time and place desires a full and beautiful life, just and good, a life that is not threatened by death but can still mature and grow to fullness. The person is like a traveler who, crossing the deserts of life, thirsts for the living water: gushing and fresh, capable of quenching deep desire for light, love, beauty, and peace. We all feel this desire! And Jesus gives us this living water: he is the Holy Spirit, who proceeds from the Father and whom Jesus pours out into our hearts. "I came that they may have life, and have it abundantly," Jesus tells us (John 10:10).

At this point we may ask ourselves: why can this water quench our thirst deep down? We know that water is essential to life; without water we die. It quenches, washes, and makes the earth fertile. In the letter to the Romans we find these words: "God's love has been poured into our hearts through the Holy Spirit who has been given to us" (Rom. 5:5). The "living water" is the Holy Spirit, the gift of the Risen One who dwells in us, purifies us, illuminates us, renews us, and transforms us because he makes us participants in the very life of God that is Love. That is why, the apostle Paul says, the Christian's life is moved by the Holy Spirit and by his fruit, which is "love, joy, peace, patience, kindness, goodness, faithfulness, gentleness, self-control"

(Gal. 5:22–23). *The Holy Spirit introduces us to divine life as "children in the only begotten Son."*

The Holy Spirit teaches us to see with the eyes of Christ, to live life as Christ lived, to understand life as Christ understood it. That is why the living water, who is the Holy Spirit, quenches our life, why he tells us that we are loved by God as children, that we can love God as his children, and that by his grace we can live as children of God, like Jesus.

And we, do we listen to the Holy Spirit? What does the Holy Spirit tell us? He says, *God loves you.* He tells us this. *God loves you, God likes you.* Do we truly love God and others, as Jesus does? Let us allow ourselves to be guided by the Holy Spirit, let us allow him to speak to our hearts and say this to us: God is love, God is waiting for us; God is Father and loves us as a true father loves; he loves us truly, and only the Holy Spirit can tell us this in our hearts. Let us hear the Holy Spirit, let us listen to the Holy Spirit, and may we move forward on this path of love, mercy, and forgiveness.

But there's more: the Holy Spirit also lets us speak to men through *prophecy*, making us humble and docile channels of God's Word. Prophecy is made with candor, to openly demonstrate the contradictions and injustices, but always with compassion and constructive intent. Charged with the Spirit of love, we can be signs and instruments of God, who loves, who serves, who gives life.

So how does the Holy Spirit act in our life and in the life of the Church in order to guide us to the Truth? First of all, he recalls and impresses in the hearts of believers the words Jesus spoke and, through these very words, the law of God—as the prophets of the Old Testament had foretold—is engraved in our hearts and becomes within us a criterion for evaluation in decisions and for guidance in our daily actions; it becomes a principle to live by. Ezekiel's great prophecy is brought about: "You shall be clean from all your uncleanness, and from all your idols I will cleanse you. A new heart I will give you, and a new spirit I will put within you. . . . And I will put my spirit within you, and cause you to walk in my statutes and be careful to observe my ordinances" (Ezek. 36:25–27). Indeed, it is in our inmost depths that our actions come into being; it is the heart itself that must be converted to God, and the Holy Spirit transforms it when we open ourselves to him.

Some in Jerusalem would have liked Jesus' disciples, frozen in fear, to remain locked inside so as not to create *confusion*. Even today, many would like this from the Christians. Instead, the risen Lord pushes them into the world: "As the Father has sent me, even so I send you" (John 20:21). The Church of Pentecost is a Church that won't submit to being powerless, too "distilled." No, she doesn't submit to this! She doesn't want to be a decoration. She is a Church that doesn't hesitate to go out, meet the people, proclaim the message that's been entrusted to her, even if that message disturbs or unsettles the conscience, even if that message perhaps brings problems and sometimes leads to martyrdom. She is born one and universal, with a distinct identity, but open, a Church that embraces the world but doesn't seize it. She sets it free but embraces it like the colonnade in this Square: two arms that open to receive but that don't close to detain. We Christians are free, and the Church wants us free!

In truth, the Church shows her fidelity to the Holy Spirit in as much as she does not try to control or tame him. And the Church shows herself also when she rejects the temptation to look only inward. We Christians become true missionary disciples, able to challenge consciences, when we throw off our defensiveness and allow ourselves to be led by the Spirit. He is freshness, imagination, and newness.

*Newness* always makes us a bit fearful, because we feel more secure if we have everything under control, if we are the ones who build, program, and plan our lives in accordance with our own ideas, our own comfort, our own preferences. This is also the case when it comes to God. Often we follow him, we accept him, but only up to a certain point. It is hard to abandon ourselves to him with complete trust, allowing the Holy Spirit to be the soul and guide of our lives in our every decision. We fear that God may force us to strike out on new paths and leave behind our all too narrow, closed, and selfish horizons in order to become open to his own. Yet throughout the history of salvation, whenever God reveals himself, he brings newness—God always brings newness—and demands our complete trust: Noah, mocked by all, builds an ark and is saved; Abram leaves his land with only a promise in hand; Moses stands up to the might of Pharaoh and leads his people to freedom; the apostles, huddled fearfully in the Upper Room, go forth with courage to proclaim the Gospel.

The Holy Spirit is the soul of *mission*. The events that took place in Jerusalem about two thousand years ago are not far removed from us; they are events that affect us and become a lived experience in each of us. The Pentecost of the Upper Room in Jerusalem is the beginning, a beginning that endures. The Holy Spirit is the supreme gift of the risen Christ to his apostles, yet he wants that gift to reach everyone. In John's Gospel, Jesus says: "I will ask the Father, and he will give you another Advocate to remain with you forever" (14:16). It is the Paraclete Spirit, the "Comforter," who grants us the courage to take to the streets of the world, bringing the Gospel! The Holy Spirit makes us look to the horizon and drives us to the very outskirts of existence in order to proclaim life in Jesus Christ.

In intimacy with God and in listening to his Word, little by little we put aside our own way of thinking, which is most often dictated by our tunnel vision, by our prejudice, and by our ambitions, and we learn instead to ask the Lord, What is your desire? What is your will? What pleases you? In this way a deep, almost *connatural harmony* in the Spirit grows and develops within us, and we experience how true the words of Jesus are that are reported in the Gospel of Matthew: "Do not be anxious how you are to speak or what you are to say; for what you are to say will be given to you in that hour; for it is not you who speak but the spirit of your Father speaking through you" (10:19–20). It is the Spirit who counsels us, but we have to make room for the Spirit, so that he may counsel us. And to give space is to pray, to pray that he come and help us always.

Three ideas: *Go, do not be afraid,* and *serve. Go, do not be afraid,* and *serve.* If you follow these three ideas, you will experience that the one who evangelizes is evangelized, and the one who transmits the joy of faith receives more joy. Do not be afraid to be generous with Christ, to bear witness to his gospel. When God sends the prophet Jeremiah, he gives him the power to "pluck up and to break down, to destroy and to overthrow, to build and to plant" (Jer. 1:10). It is the same for you. Bringing the gospel is bringing God's power to pluck up and break down evil and violence, to destroy and overthrow the barriers of selfishness, intolerance, and hatred, so as to build a new world. Jesus Christ is counting on you! The Church is counting on you! The pope is counting on you! May Mary, Mother of Jesus and our Mother, always accompany you with her tenderness: "Go and make disciples of all nations."

Fear of the Lord is the gift of the Holy Spirit through whom we are reminded of how small we are before God and of his love, and that our good lies in humble, respectful, and trusting self-abandonment into his hands. This is fear of the Lord: abandonment in the goodness of our Father who loves us so much.

Fear of the Lord allows us to be aware that everything comes from grace and that our true strength lies solely in following the Lord Jesus and in allowing the Father to bestow upon us his goodness and his mercy. [Fear of the Lord helps us] open the heart, so that the goodness and mercy of God may come to us. This is what the Holy Spirit does through the gift of fear of the Lord: he opens hearts. The heart opens so that forgiveness, mercy, goodness, and the caress of the Father may come to us, for as children we are infinitely loved.

Yet, we should take care, for the gift of God, the gift of fear of the Lord, is also an "alarm" against the obstinacy of sin. When a person lives in evil, when one blasphemes against God, when one exploits others or tyrannizes them, when he lives only for money, for vanity, for power, or pride, then the holy fear of God sends us a warning: be careful! With all this power, with all this money, with all your pride, with all your vanity, you will not be happy. No one can take it with [him or her] to the other side: not the money, power, vanity, or pride. Nothing! We can take only the love that God the Father gives us, God's embrace, accepted and received by us with love. And we can take what we have done for others. Take care not to place your hope in money or pride, power or vanity, because they can promise you nothing good!

I would like to add a word about another particular work situation that concerns me: I am referring to what we could define as "slave labor," work that enslaves. How many people worldwide are victims of this type of slavery, when the person is at the service of his or her work, while work should offer a service to people so they may have dignity? I ask my brothers and sisters in the faith and all men and women of good will for a decisive choice to combat the trafficking in persons, in which "slave labor" exists.

I am thinking of those who live off human trafficking or slave labor; do you think these people who traffic persons, who exploit people through slave labor, have love for God in their hearts? No, they haven't fear of the Lord, and they are not happy. They are not. I am thinking of those who manufacture weapons for fomenting wars; just think about what kind of job this is. I am certain that if I were to ask, "How many of you manufacture weapons?" there would be no one, no one. These weapons manufacturers don't come to hear the Word of God! These people manufacture death; they are merchants of death, and they make death into a piece of merchandise. May fear of the Lord make them understand that one day all things will come to an end and they will have to give account to God.

Fear of the Lord, therefore, does not make of us Christians who are shy and submissive; [rather, it] stirs in us courage and strength! It is a gift that makes of us Christians who are convinced, enthusiastic, who aren't submissive to the Lord out of fear but because we are moved and conquered by his love! To be conquered by the love of God! This is a beautiful thing. To allow ourselves to be conquered by this love of a Father, who loves us so, loves us with all his heart.

Dear friends, Psalm 34 tells us to pray like this: "This poor man cried, and the Lord heard him, and saved him out of all his troubles. The angel of the Lord encamps around those who fear him, and delivers them" (6–7).

Let us ask the Lord for the grace to unite our voice to that of the poor, to welcome the gift of fear of the Lord and to be able to recognize ourselves, together with them, as cloaked in the mercy and love of God, who is our Father, our dad. Let it be.

# 10

# The Church, God's Great Family

It is not possible "to love Christ but without the Church, to listen to Christ but not the Church, to belong to Christ but outside the Church." For the Church is herself God's great family, which brings Christ to us. Our faith is not an abstract doctrine or philosophy, but a vital and full relationship with a person: Jesus Christ, the only begotten Son of God, who became man, was put to death, rose from the dead to save us, and is now living in our midst. Where can we encounter him? We encounter him in the Church, in our hierarchical Holy Mother Church. It is the Church that says today: "Behold the Lamb of God"; it is the Church that proclaims him; it is in the Church that Jesus continues to accomplish his acts of grace, which are the sacraments.

Christ is the living temple of the Father, and Christ himself builds his "spiritual house": the Church, not made of material stones but rather of "living stones," which we are. The apostle Paul said to the Christians of Ephesus: you are "built upon the foundation of the apostles and prophets, Christ Jesus himself being the cornerstone, in whom the whole structure is joined together and grows into a holy temple in the Lord; in whom you also are built . . . for a dwelling place of God in the Spirit" (Eph. 2:20–22). This is a beautiful thing! We are the living stones of God's building, profoundly united to Christ who is the keystone and also the one who sustains us. What does this mean? It means that we are the temple—we are the living Church, the living temple—and with us when we are together is also the Holy Spirit, who helps us grow as Church. We are not alone, for we are the People of God: this is the Church!

So what is the Church born from? She is born from the supreme act of love of the cross, from the pierced side of Jesus from which flowed blood and water, a symbol of the sacrament of the Eucharist and of baptism. The lifeblood of God's family, of the Church, is God's love, which is actualized in loving him and oth-

> *The lifeblood of God's family, of the Church, is God's love, which is actualized in loving him and others—all others—without distinction or reservation.*

ers—all others—without distinction or reservation. The Church is a family in which we love and are loved.

The Church's activity and mission are expressions of her motherhood. For she is like a mother who tenderly holds Jesus and gives him to everyone with joy and generosity. No manifestation of Christ, even the most mystical, can ever be detached from the flesh and blood of the Church, from the historical concreteness of the Body of Christ. Without the Church, Jesus Christ ends up as an idea, a moral teaching, a feeling. Without the Church, our relationship with Christ would be at the mercy of our imagination, our interpretations, and our moods.

What is God's plan? It is to make of us all a single family of his children, in which each person feels that God is close and feels loved by him, as in the Gospel parable, feels the warmth of being God's family. The Church is rooted in this great plan. She is not an organization established by an agreement between a few people, but—as Pope Benedict XVI has so often reminded us—she is a work of God, born precisely from this loving design, which is gradually brought about in history. The Church is born from God's wish to call all people to communion with him, to friendship with him, indeed, to share in his own divine life as his sons and daughters. The very word *iglesia* [translated to "church" in English], from the Greek *ekklesia*, means "convocation": God convokes us, he impels us to come out of our individualism, from our tendency to close ourselves into ourselves, and he calls us to belong to his family.

The Church does not rest solely beneath the shadow of our steeple; rather, she embraces a vast number of peoples and nations who profess the same faith, are nourished by the same Eucharist, and are served by the same pastors. To feel that we are in communion with the whole Church, with all of the Catholic communities of the world great and small—this is beautiful! And then, to feel we are all on mission, great and small communities alike, that we all must open our doors and go out for the sake of the Gospel. Let us ask ourselves then, what do I do in order to communicate to others the joy of encountering the Lord, the joy of belonging to the Church? Proclaiming and bearing witness to the faith is not the work of the few; it also concerns me, you, each one of us!

What can I, a weak fragile sinner, do? God says to you, Do not be afraid of holiness; do not be afraid to aim high, to let yourself be loved and purified by God. Do not be afraid to let yourself be guided by the Holy Spirit. Let us be infected by the holiness of God. Every Christian is called to sanctity, and sanctity does not consist especially in doing extraordinary things but in allowing God to act. [Sanctity] is the meeting of our weakness with the strength of God's grace; it is having faith in his action that allows us to live in charity, to do everything with joy and humility, for the glory of God and as a service to our neighbor. There is a celebrated saying by the French writer Léon Bloy, who in the last moments of his life said, "The only real sadness in life is not becoming a saint." Let us not lose the hope of holiness, let us follow this path. Do we want to be saints? The Lord awaits us, with open arms; he waits to accompany us on the path to sanctity. Let us live in the joy of our faith, let us allow ourselves to be loved by the Lord . . . in prayer let us ask for this gift from God, for ourselves and for others.

We can say that [the Church] is like family life. In the family, everything that enables us to grow, to mature, and to live is given to each of us. We cannot grow up by ourselves, we cannot journey on our own, in isolation; rather, we journey and grow in a community, in a family. And so it is in the Church! In the Church we can listen to the Word of God with the assurance that it is the message the Lord has given us. In the Church we can encounter the Lord in the sacraments, which are the open windows through which the light of God is given to us, streams from which we can draw God's very life. In the Church we learn to live in the communion and love that come from God. Each one of us can ask himself or herself today: How do I live in the Church? When I go to church, is it as though I were at the stadium, at a football match? Is it as though I were at the cinema? No, it is something else. How do I go to church? How do I receive the gifts that the Church offers me to grow and mature as a Christian? Do I participate in the life of the community, or do I go to church and withdraw into my own problems, isolating myself from others? In this first sense, the Church is catholic because she is everyone's home. Everyone is a child of the Church, and in her all find their home.

One's thought goes in the first place, with gratitude, to *those who went before us* and who welcomed us into the Church. No one becomes Christian on his or her own. Is that clear? No one becomes Christian by him- or herself. Christians are not made in a laboratory. A Christian is part of a people who comes from afar. The Christian belongs to a people called the Church, and this Church is what makes him or her Christian, on the day of baptism, and then in the course of catechesis, and so on. But no one, no one becomes Christian on his or her own. If we believe, if we know how to pray, if we acknowledge the Lord and can listen to his Word, if we feel him close to us and recognize him in our brothers and sisters, it is because others, before us, lived the faith and then transmitted it to us.

Our witness is to make others understand what it means to be Christian. Let us ask not to be a source of scandal. Let us ask for the gift of faith, so that we can understand how, despite our smallness and our poverty, the Lord has made us a true vehicle of grace and a visible sign of his love for all humanity. We can become a cause of scandal, yes. But we can also become a cause of witness, by saying with our life what Jesus wants of us.

# 11

# Mary, Model of Union with Christ

———————

Mary is so closely united to Jesus because she received from him the knowledge of the heart, the knowledge of faith, nourished by her experience as a mother and by her close relationship with her Son. The Blessed Virgin is the woman of faith who made room for God in her heart and in her plans; she is the believer capable of perceiving in the gift of her Son the coming of that "fullness of time" (Gal. 4:4) in which God, by choosing the humble path of human existence, entered personally into the history of salvation. That is why Jesus cannot be understood without his mother.

At the message of the angel, Mary does not hide her surprise. It is the astonishment of realizing that God, to become man, had chosen her, a simple maid of Nazareth. Not someone who lived in a palace amid power and riches, nor one who had done extraordinary things, but simply someone who was open to God and who put her trust in him, even without understanding everything: "Here I am, the servant of the Lord; let it be with me according to your word" (Luke 1:38). That was her answer. God constantly surprises us, he bursts our categories, he wreaks havoc with our plans. And he tells us: "Trust me, do not be afraid, let yourself be surprised, leave yourself behind and follow me!"

At the Annunciation, the messenger of God calls Mary "full of grace" and reveals this plan to her. Mary answers yes, and from that moment her faith receives new light. It is concentrated on Jesus, the Son of God, who from her took flesh and in whom all the promises of salvation history are fulfilled. Mary's faith is the fulfillment of Israel's faith; the whole journey, the whole path of that people awaiting redemption, is contained in her, and it is in this sense that she is the model of the Church's faith, which has Christ, the incarnation of God's infinite love, as its center.

How did Mary live this faith? She lived it out in the simplicity of the thousand daily tasks and worries of every mother, such as providing food and clothing, caring for the house. . . . It was precisely Our Lady's normal life that served as the basis for the unique relationship and profound dialogue that unfolded between her and God, between her and her Son. Mary's yes, already perfect from the start, grew until the hour of the cross. There her motherhood opened to embrace every one of us, our lives, so as to guide us to her Son. As Jesus' first and perfect disciple, Mary lived perpetually immersed in the mystery of God-made-man by contemplating all things in her heart in the light of the Holy Spirit, in order to understand and live out the will of God.

> *It was precisely Our Lady's normal life that served as the basis for the unique relationship and profound dialogue that unfolded between her and God, between her and her Son.*

[W]e can also praise [God] and glorify him, like the shepherds who came away from Bethlehem with a song of thanksgiving after seeing the child and his young mother (Luke 2:16). The two were together, just as they were together at Calvary, because *Christ and his mother are inseparable.* There is a very close relationship between them, as there is between every child and his or her mother. The flesh (*caro*) of Christ—which, as Tertullian says, is the hinge (*cardo*) of our salvation—was knit together in the womb of Mary (see Ps. 139:13). This inseparability is also clear from the fact that Mary, chosen beforehand to be the Mother of the Redeemer, shared intimately in his entire mission, remaining at her Son's side to the end on Calvary.

*Mary [is] the model of charity.* In what way is Mary a living example of love for the Church? Let us think of the readiness she showed toward her cousin Elizabeth. In visiting her, the Virgin Mary brought not only material help—she brought this too—but she also brought Jesus, who was already alive in her womb. Bringing Jesus into that house meant bringing joy, the fullness of joy. Elizabeth and Zechariah were rejoicing at a pregnancy that had seemed impossible at their age, but it was the young Mary who brought them the fullness of joy, the joy that comes from Jesus and from the Holy Spirit, and is expressed by gratuitous charity, by sharing with, helping, and understanding others.

*Mary [is] the model of union with Christ.* The life of the Holy Virgin was the life of a woman of her people: Mary prayed, she worked, and she went to the synagogue. . . . But every action was carried out in perfect union with Jesus. This union finds its culmination on Calvary: here Mary is united to the Son in the martyrdom of her heart and in the offering of his life to the Father for the salvation of humanity. Our Lady shared in the pain of the Son and accepted with him the will of the Father, in that obedience that bears fruit, that grants the true victory over evil and death.

Mary says, "My soul glorifies the Lord." Today, the Church too sings this in every part of the world. This song is particularly strong in places where the Body of Christ is suffering the Passion. For us Christians, wherever the cross is, there is hope, always. If there is no hope, we are not Christian. That is why I like to say, "Do not allow yourselves to be robbed of hope." May we not be robbed of hope, because this strength is a grace, a gift from God that carries us forward with our eyes fixed on heaven. And Mary is always there, near those communities, our brothers and sisters; she accompanies them, suffers with them, and sings the Magnificatof hope with them.

Mary also experienced the martyrdom of the cross: the martyrdom of her heart, the martyrdom of her soul. She lived her son's Passion to the depths of her soul. She was fully united to him in his death, and so she was given the gift of resurrection. Christ is the firstfruits from the dead, and Mary is the first of the redeemed, the first of "those who are in Christ." She is our Mother, but we can also say that she is our representative, our sister, our eldest sister. She is the first of the redeemed, who has arrived in heaven.

Along our path, which is often difficult, we are not alone. We are so many, we are a people, and the gaze of Our Lady helps us look at one another as brothers and sisters. Let us look upon one another in a more fraternal way! Mary teaches us to have that gaze that strives to welcome, to accompany, and to protect. Let us learn to look at one another beneath Mary's maternal gaze! There are people we instinctively consider "less" and who instead are in greater need: the most abandoned, the sick, those who have nothing to live on, those who do not know Jesus, youth who find themselves in difficulty, young people who cannot find work.

Mary has always been present in the hearts of the Christian people, in their piety and above all in their pilgrimage of faith. "The Church journeys through time . . . and on this journey she proceeds along the path already trodden by the Virgin Mary" (*Redemptoris Mater*, 2). Our journey of faith is the same as that of Mary, and so we feel that she is particularly close to us. As far as faith—the hinge of the Christian life—is concerned, the Mother of God shared our condition. She had to take the same path as we do, a path sometimes difficult and obscure. She had to advance in the "pilgrimage of faith" (*Lumen gentium*, 58).

Our pilgrimage of faith has been inseparably linked to Mary ever since Jesus, dying on the cross, gave her to us as our Mother, saying, "Behold your Mother!" (John 19:27). These words serve as a testament, bequeathing to the world a Mother. From that moment on, the Mother of God also became our Mother! When the faith of the disciples was most tested by difficulties and uncertainties, Jesus entrusted them to Mary, who was the first to believe and whose faith would never fail. The "woman" became our Mother when she lost her divine Son. Her sorrowing heart was enlarged to make room for all men and women—all, whether good or bad—and she loves them as she loved Jesus. The woman who at the wedding at Cana in Galilee gave her faith-filled cooperation so that the wonders of God could be displayed in the world, at Calvary kept alive the flame of faith in the resurrection of her Son, and she communicates this with maternal affection to each and every person. Mary becomes in this way a source of hope and true joy.

The Mother of the Redeemer goes before us and continually strengthens us in faith, in our vocation, and in our mission. By her example of humility and openness to God's will she helps us transmit our faith in a joyful procla-mation of the Gospel to all, without reservation. In this way our mission will be fruitful, because it is modeled on the motherhood of Mary. To her let us entrust our journey of faith, the desires of our heart, our needs and the needs of the whole world, especially of those who hunger and thirst for justice and peace, and for God.

Let us not be afraid to go out and look upon our brothers and sisters with Our Lady's gaze. She invites us to be true brothers and sisters. And let us never allow something or someone to come between us and Our Lady's gaze. Mother, grant us your gaze! May no one hide from it! May our child-like heart know how to defend itself against the many "windbags" who make false promises, from those who have a gaze greedy for an easy life and full of promises that cannot be fulfilled. May they not rob us of Mary's gaze, which is full of tenderness, which gives us strength and builds solidarity among us. Let us say together, Mother, grant us your gaze!

# 12

# The Saints, Anchored in Hope

The Feast of All Saints that we are celebrating today reminds us that the goal of our existence is not death, it is paradise! The apostle John writes, "It does not yet appear what we shall be, but we know that when he appears we shall be like him, for we shall see him as he is" (1 John 3:2). The saints—who are the friends of God—assure us of this promise that does not disappoint. During their earthly existence they lived in profound communion with God. In the faces of the humblest and least of our brothers, the smallest and most despised brothers, they saw the face of God, and now they contemplate him face to face in his glorious beauty.

And on All Saints' Day and the first day that we commemorate the faithful departed, we need to think a little about this hope that accompanies us in life. The first Christians depicted hope with an anchor, as though life were an anchor cast on heaven's shores, with all of us journeying to that shore, clinging to the anchor's rope. This is a beautiful image of hope: to have our hearts anchored there, where our beloved predecessors are, where the saints are, where Jesus is, where God is. This is the hope that does not disappoint; today and tomorrow are days of hope.

Through this feast, the saints give us a message. They tell us, "Trust in the Lord because the Lord does not disappoint!" He never disappoints, he is a good friend always at our side. Through their witness the saints encourage us to not be afraid of going against the tide or of being misunderstood and mocked when we speak about Jesus and the Gospel. By their lives the saints show us that the one who stays faithful to God and to his Word experiences the comfort of God's love on this earth and then a "hundredfold" in eternity. This is what we hope for and ask of the Lord, for our deceased brothers and sisters. With her wisdom the Church has placed the Feast of All Saints and All Souls' Day near each other. May our prayer of praise to God and veneration of the blessed spirits join with the prayer of suffrage for the souls of those who have preceded us in the passage from this world to eternal life.

Saints are people who for love of God did not put conditions on him in their lives; they were not hypocrites but spent their lives at the service of others. They suffered much adversity but without hate. The saints never hated. Understand this well: love is of God. Then from whom does hatred come? Hatred does not come from God but from the devil! And the saints removed themselves from the devil; the saints are men and women who have joy in their hearts, and they spread it to others. Never hate but serve others, [especially] the most needy; pray and live in joy. This is the way of holiness!

Being holy is not a privilege for the few, as if someone had a large inheritance; in baptism we all have an inheritance, which is the ability to become saints. Holiness is a vocation for everyone. Thus we all are called to walk on the path of holiness, and this path has a name and a face: the face of Jesus Christ. He teaches us to become saints. In the Gospel he shows us the way, the way of the Beatitudes (see Matt. 5:1–12).

If we are rooted in the source of Love, which is God, then a reciprocal movement also occurs: from brothers to God. The experience of fraternal communion leads me to communion with God. Union among us leads to union with God; it leads us to this bond with God who is our Father. This is the second aspect of the communion of saints I would like to underline: *our faith needs the support of others*, especially in difficult moments. If we are united, our faith becomes stronger. How beautiful it is to support one another in the wonderful adventure of faith.

> *Being holy is not a privilege for the few, as if someone had a large inheritance; in baptism we all have an inheritance, which is the ability to become saints. Holiness is a vocation for everyone.*

The communion of saints goes *beyond earthly life, beyond death, and endures forever*. This union among us goes beyond this life and continues in the next life; it is a spiritual communion born in baptism and not broken by death, but, thanks to the risen Christ, is destined to find its fullness in eternal life. There is a deep and indissoluble bond between those who are still pilgrims in this world—us—and those who have crossed the threshold of death and entered eternity. All baptized persons here on earth, the souls in purgatory, and all the blessed who are already in paradise make one great family. This communion between earth and heaven is realized especially in intercessory prayer.

We should all ask ourselves: How do I bear witness to Christ through my faith? Do I have the courage of Peter and the other apostles, to think, to choose, and to live as a Christian, obedient to God? To be sure, the testimony of faith comes in very many forms, just as in a great fresco there is a variety of colors and shades; yet they are all important, even those that do not stand out. In God's great plan, every detail is important, even yours, even my humble little witness, even the hidden witness of those who live their faith with simplicity in every-day family relationships, work relationships, and friendships.

There are the saints of every day, the "hidden" saints, a sort of "middle class of holiness," as a French author said, that middle class of holiness to which we can all belong. But in different parts of the world, there are also those who suffer, like Peter and the apostles, on account of the Gospel; there are those who give their lives in order to remain faithful to Christ by means of a witness marked by the shedding of their blood. Let us all remember this: one cannot proclaim the Gospel of Jesus without the tangible witness of one's life. Those who listen to us and observe us must be able to see in our actions what they hear from our lips, and so give glory to God! I am thinking now of some advice that St. Francis of Assisi gave his brothers: preach the Gospel, and, if necessary, use words. Preaching with your life, with your witness.

The saints are not supermen, nor were they born perfect. They are like us, like each one of us. They are people who, before reaching the glory of heaven, lived normal lives with joys and sorrows, struggles and hopes. What changed their lives? When they recognized God's love, they followed it with all their heart without reserve or hypocrisy. They spent their lives serving others; they endured suffering and adversity without hatred and responded to evil with good, spreading joy and peace. This is the life of a saint.

It is happening today. It seems that these people, these children who are hungry and sick, do not seem to count. It's as if they were of a different species, as if they were not even human. And this multitude is before God and asks, "Salvation, please! Peace, please! Bread, please! Work, please! Children and grandparents, please! Young people with the dignity of being able to work, please!" Among these are also those who are persecuted for their faith; there "then one of the elders addressed me, saying, 'who are these, clothed in white, and when have they come?' . . . 'These are they who have come out of great tribulation; they have washed their robes and made them white in the blood of the Lamb'" (Rev. 7:13–14). And today, without exaggeration, today on the Feast of All Saints I would like us to think of all these, the unknown saints. Sinners like us, worse off than us, destroyed. May we think of this multitude of people who are in great distress. Most of the world is in tribulation. And the Lord sanctifies this people, sinners like us, but he sanctifies these people in tribulation.

In fact, the Kingdom of Heaven is for those who do not place their security in material things but in love for God, for those who have simple, humble hearts and who do not presume to be just and do not judge others. The Kingdom of Heaven is for those who know how to suffer with those who suffer and how to rejoice when others rejoice. They are not violent but merciful and strive to be instruments for reconciliation and peace. Saints, whether men or women, are instruments for reconciliation and peace; they are always helping people become reconciled and helping to bring about peace. Thus holiness is beautiful; it is a beautiful path!

# Endnotes

**Page 1**: Jesus Christ is the face of the Father's mercy. . . . Papal Bull, April 11, 2015. (www.vatican.va).

**Page 7**: In the Gospel the essential thing is *mercy*. . . . General Audience, September 10, 2014. (www.vatican.va).

**Page 7**: The Church is Mother, by teaching her children works of mercy. . . . General Audience, September 10, 2014. (www.vatican.va).

**Page 7**: Someone might say to me, "But Father, I don't have time," . . . General Audience, March 27, 2013. (www.vatican.va).

**Page 8**: When we enter our hearts . . . Homily, Third Sunday of Lent, March 8, 2015. (www.vatican.va).

**Page 8**: The Church, which is holy, does not reject sinners . . . General Audience, October 2, 2013. (www.vatican.va).

**Page 9**: The prophet Hosea says, "I have walked with you . . . General Audience, June 18, 2014. (www.vatican.va).

**Page 9**: Dear brothers and sisters, the Lord never tires . . . Homily, Basilica of Santa Sabina, February 18, 2015. (www.vatican.va).

**Page 10**: Celebrating the sacrament of reconciliation . . . General Audience, February 19, 2014. (www.vatican.va).

**Page 10**: In the Church, the God we encounter . . . General Audience, October 2, 2013. (www.vatican.va).

**Page 10**: [The father in the parable] . . . General Audience, March 27, 2013. (www.vatican.va).

**Page 10**: One might say: I confess only to God. . . . General Audience, February 19, 2014. (www.vatican.va).

Page 11: The sacrament of reconciliation is a sacrament of healing. . . . General Audience, February 19, 2014. (www.vatican.va).

Page 11: The forgiveness of our sins is not something . . . General Audience, February 19, 2014. (www.vatican.va).

Page 11: Jesus gave the apostles the power to forgive sins. . . . General Audience, November 20, 2013. (www.vatican.va).

Page 12: Do not be afraid of confession! . . . General Audience, February 19, 2014. (www.vatican.va).

Page 12: Perhaps many do not understand the ecclesial dimension . . . General Audience, November 20, 2013. (www.vatican.va).

Page 12: There is a biblical icon that expresses, . . . General Audience, February 26, 2014. (www.vatican.va).

Page 13: This mandate is repeated . . . General Audience, February 26, 2014. (www.vatican.va).

Page 13: But when someone is sick, and we say, . . . General Audience, February 26, 2014. (www.vatican.va).

Page 14: But the greatest comfort comes from . . . General Audience, February 26, 2014. (www.vatican.va).

Page 14: And I tell you, truly: it grieves me . . . Homily, Vatican Basilica, May 11, 2014. (www.vatican.va).

Page 14: They all have something in common . . . Address, St. Peter's Square, May 18, 2013. (www.vatican.va).

Page 15: If one understands his brother . . . Homily, February 16, 2014. (www.vatican.va).

Page 15: Think of the gossip [among Jesus' followers] . . . Homily, Fifth Sunday of Lent, March 17, 2013. (www.vatican.va).

Page 16: I would like to emphasize one other thing . . . Homily, Basilica of Saint John Lateran, Divine Mercy Sunday, April 7, 2013. (www.vatican.va).

Page 16: This is important: the courage to trust in Jesus' mercy, . . . Homily, Basilica of Saint John Lateran, Divine Mercy Sunday, April 7, 2013. (www.vatican.va).

Page 17: Jesus challenges us . . . to take seriously . . . Message of Pope Francis for the Twenty-Ninth World Youth Day, January 21, 2014. (www.vatican.va).

Page 19: The origin of the darkness . . . Homily, Vatican Basilica, December 24, 2014. (www.vatican.va).

**Page 19:** In the Bible, God always appears . . . Address, Vatican Basilica, November 23, 2013. (www.vatican.va).

**Page 20:** The Word of God pitched his tent among us, . . . Angelus, St. Peter's Square, January 5, 2014. (www.vatican.va).

**Page 20:** Jesus is all mercy. . . . Angelus, St. Peter's Square, September 15, 2013. (www.vatican.va).

**Page 20:** [Remember] Peter: three times he denied Jesus . . . Homily, Basilica of Saint John Lateran, Divine Mercy Sunday, April 7, 2013. (www.vatican.va).

**Page 20:** Jesus, when on the cross, . . . Morning Meditation in the chapel of the Domus Sanctae Marthae, June 28, 2013. (www.vatican.va).

**Page 21:** The Gospel presents to us the episode . . . Angelus, St. Peter's Square, March 17, 2013. (www.vatican.va).

**Page 21:** [T]he apostle Thomas personally experiences . . . Homily, Basilica of Saint John Lateran, Divine Mercy Sunday, April 7, 2013. (www.vatican.va).

**Page 21:** Let us think too of the two disciples . . . Homily, Basilica of Saint John Lateran, Divine Mercy Sunday, April 7, 2013. (www.vatican.va).

**Page 22:** Our lives are sometimes similar to that . . . Angelus, St. Peter's Square, Fourth Sunday of Lent, March 30, 2014. (www.vatican.va).

**Page 22:** The liturgy proposes several Gospel parables . . . Angelus, St. Peter's Square, July 20, 2014. (www.vatican.va).

**Page 23:** The teaching of the parable is twofold . . . . Angelus, St. Peter's Square, July 20, 2014. (www.vatican.va).

**Page 23:** And here we arrive at the second theme . . . Angelus, St. Peter's Square, July 20, 2014. (www.vatican.va).

**Page 23:** With patience and mercy he gazes . . . Angelus, St. Peter's Square, July 20, 2014. (www.vatican.va).

**Page 23:** The field owner's attitude . . . Angelus, St. Peter's Square, July 20, 2014. (www.vatican.va).

**Page 23:** In the end, in fact, evil will be removed . . . Angelus, St. Peter's Square, July 20, 2014. (www.vatican.va).

**Page 24:** The Lord always chooses his way . . . Morning Meditation in the chapel of the Domus Sanctae Marthae, June 28, 2013. (www.vatican.va).

**Page 24:** The Lord takes his time. . . . Morning Meditation in the chapel of the Domus Sanctae Marthae, June 28, 2013. (www.vatican.va).

**Page 24:** God asks us for faithfulness . . . Morning Meditation in the chapel of the Domus Sanctae Marthae, November 28, 2013. (www.vatican.va).

**Page 25:** [Listening] always demands the patience . . . *Evanglii Gaudium*, no. 171. (www.vatican.va).

**Page 25:** The Lord who walks with God . . . Morning Meditation in the chapel of the Domus Sanctae Marthae, September 8, 2014. (www.vatican.va).

**Page 25:** And above all, a love that is patient . . . Homily, St. Peter's Square, October 27, 2013. (www.vatican.va).

**Page 25:** "But, father, I work in a factory . . . General Audience, November 19, 2014. (www.vatican.va).

**Page 26:** God's love always comes . . . Angelus, St. Peter's Square, January 6, 2014. (www.vatican.va).

**Page 27:** The dominant sentiment that shines . . . *Regina Caeli*, St. Peter's Square, Easter Monday, April 21, 2014. (www.vatican.va).

**Page 27:** All divine revelation is the fruit . . . Homily, Vatican Basilica, Altar of the Chair, November 3, 2014. (www.vatican.va).

**Page 27:** [In] the profession of faith . . . General Audience, April 3, 2013. (www.vatican.va).

**Page 28:** But let us return to the Gospel . . . Homily, Vatican Basilica, Holy Saturday, March 30, 2013. (www.vatican.va).

**Page 28:** After his appearances to the women . . . General Audience, April 3, 2013. (www.vatican.va).

**Page 28:** Jesus is not dead, he has risen . . . Homily, Vatican Basilica, Holy Saturday, March 30, 2013. (www.vatican.va).

**Page 29:** We need to hear ourselves repeat the angels' . . . General Audience, April 23, 2014. (www.vatican.va).

**Page 29:** And this is a message meant for me . . . Homily, Vatican Basilica, Holy Saturday, March 30, 2013. (www.vatican.va).

**Page 29:** John's Gospel tells us that Jesus appeared twice . . . *Regina Caeli*, Divine Mercy Sunday, April 7, 2013. (www.vatican.va).

**Page 30:** Jesus, in the New Testament . . . General Audience, December 4, 2013. (www.vatican.va).

**Page 30:** What does it mean for the Church . . . Angelus, St. Peter's Square, January 19, 2014. (www.vatican.va).

**Page 31:** It is not easy to be open . . . General Audience, April 23, 2014. (www.vatican.va).

**Page 31**: *What does it mean to rise again?* . . . General Audience, December 4, 2013. (www.vatican.va).

**Page 31**: Without this faith in the death . . . General Audience, April 3, 2013. (www.vatican.va).

**Page 32**: The women encounter the newness of God. . . . Homily, Vatican Basilica, Holy Saturday, March 30, 2013. (www.vatican.va).

**Page 32**: Let us allow this experience . . . *Regina Caeli*, St. Peter's Square, Easter Monday, April 21, 2014. (www.vatican.va).

**Page 33**: Whoever experiences this becomes a witness . . . *Regina Caeli*, St. Peter's Square, Easter Monday, April 21, 2014. (www.vatican.va).

**Page 33**: After the death of the Master . . . Homily, Vatican Basilica, Holy Saturday, April 19, 2014. (www.vatican.va).

**Page 33**: Galilee is the place where they were first called . . . Homily, Vatican Basilica, Holy Saturday, April 19, 2014. (www.vatican.va).

**Page 33**: To return to Galilee means to reread . . . Homily, Vatican Basilica, Holy Saturday, April 19, 2014. (www.vatican.va).

**Page 33**: For each of us, too, there is a Galilee . . . Homily, Vatican Basilica, Holy Saturday, April 19, 2014. (www.vatican.va).

**Page 34**: In the life of every Christian . . . Homily, Vatican Basilica, Holy Saturday, April 19, 2014. (www.vatican.va).

**Page 34**: Today, tonight, each of us can ask . . . Homily, Vatican Basilica, Holy Saturday, April 19, 2014. (www.vatican.va).

**Page 34**: The Gospel is very clear . . . Homily, Vatican Basilica, Holy Saturday, April 19, 2014. (www.vatican.va).

**Page 34**: "Galilee of the Gentiles" . . . Homily, Vatican Basilica, Holy Saturday, April 19, 2014. (www.vatican.va).

**Page 35**: Dear friends, be glad! . . . Angelus, St. Peter's Square, July 7, 2013. (www.vatican.va).

**Page 35**: The human heart desires joy . . . Angelus, St. Peter's Square, December 14, 2014. (www.vatican.va).

**Page 35**: Jesus has come to bring joy to all people . . . Angelus, St. Peter's Square, December 14, 2014. (www.vatican.va).

**Page 35**: The prophet Isaiah (40:1–5) addresses people . . . Angelus, St. Peter's Square, December 7, 2014. (www.vatican.va).

**Page 36:** Let Isaiah's call—"Comfort, comfort my people" . . . Angelus, St. Peter's Square, December 7, 2014. (www.vatican.va).

**Page 36:** Christian joy, like hope, . . . Angelus, St. Peter's Square, December 15, 2013. (www.vatican.va).

**Page 36:** [The] joy of the Gospel is not just any joy. . . . Angelus, St. Peter's Square, December 15, 2013. (www.vatican.va).

**Page 37:** He gives us the strength to go forward. . . . Angelus, St. Peter's Square, December 15, 2013 (www.vatican.va).

**Page 37:** God is God-with-us, . . . Angelus, St. Peter's Square, January 5, 2014. (www.vatican.va).

**Page 37:** And to truly welcome Jesus into . . . Angelus, St. Peter's Square, December 26, 2014. (www.vatican.va).

**Page 38:** The Gospel of Luke 15 contains three parables . . . Angelus, St. Peter's Square, September 15, 2013. (www.vatican.va).

**Page 38:** Jesus is not a lone missionary . . . Angelus, St. Peter's Square, July 7, 2013. (www.vatican.va).

**Page 38:** The Gospel of Luke tells us that those . . . Angelus, St. Peter's Square, July 7, 2013. (www.vatican.va).

**Page 39:** The Church stands entirely *within this movement* . . . Angelus, St. Peter's Square, January 6, 2014. (www.vatican.va).

**Page 39:** In Thessalonians 5:17–22 St. Paul indicates . . . Angelus, December 14, 2014. (www.vatican.va).

**Page 39:** In the Gospel of Luke 24:36–49 the disciples . . . Homily, Church of Saint Ignatius of Loyola in Campo Marzio, Rome, April 24, 2014. (www.vatican.va).

**Page 40:** It is easier to believe in a ghost . . . Homily, Church of Saint Ignatius of Loyola in Campo Marzio, Rome, April 24, 2014. (www.vatican.va).

**Page 40:** The Acts of the Apostles 3:1–9 speaks . . . Homily, Church of Saint Ignatius of Loyola in Campo Marzio, Rome, April 24, 2014. (www.vatican.va).

**Page 41:** We who are baptized, children of the Church . . . Angelus, St. Peter's Square, December 14, 2014. (www.vatican.va).

**Page 41:** Without this joy, without this glee . . . Homily, Church of Saint Ignatius of Loyola in Campo Marzio, Rome, April 24, 2014. (www.vatican.va).

**Page 41:** We cannot be messengers of God's . . . Angelus, St. Peter's Square, December 7, 2014. (www.vatican.va).

**Page 41:** The prophet Isaiah (61:1–2) suggests . . . Homily, December 14, 2014. (www.vatican.va).

**Page 42:** No one has ever heard of a sad saint . . . Angelus, St. Peter's Square, December 14, 2014. (www.vatican.va).

**Page 43:** The image of God is the married couple . . . General Audience, April 2, 2014. (www.vatican.va).

**Page 43:** When a man and a woman celebrate . . . General Audience, April 2, 2014. (www.vatican.va).

**Page 43:** The Bible uses a powerful expression . . . General Audience, April 2, 2014. (www.vatican.va).

**Page 43:** St. Paul, in the Letter to the Ephesians . . . General Audience, April 2, 2014. (www.vatican.va).

**Page 44:** There is a truly marvelous design . . . General Audience, April 2, 2014. (www.vatican.va).

**Page 44:** There are three [phrases] that always need to be said . . . General Audience, April 2, 2014. (www.vatican.va).

**Page 44:** Dear families, you know very well . . . Homily, St. Peter's Square, October 27, 2013. (www.vatican.va).

**Page 45:** How important grandparents are . . . Angelus, Central balcony of the Archbishop's Residence of St. Joaquin, Rio de Janeiro, July 26, 2013. (www.vatican.va).

**Page 45:** And Jesus heals: let yourselves be healed . . . Homily, February 8, 2015. (www.vatican.va).

**Page 45:** [W]hat is the power that unites the family? . . . Angelus, St. Peter's Square, August 11, 2013. (www.vatican.va).

**Page 46:** Each Christian family can first of all . . . General Audience, December 17, 2014. (www.vatican.va).

**Page 46:** [Jesus' love] is a love that gives value . . . Angelus, St. Peter's Square, August 11, 2013. (www.vatican.va).

**Page 46:** All families need God . . . Homily, St. Peter's Square, October 27, 2013. (www.vatican.va).

**Page 46:** We can imagine that the Virgin Mary . . . Homily, St. Peter's Square, September 28, 2014. (www.vatican.va).

**Page 47:** Before our eyes we can picture Mother Mary . . . Homily, Vatican Basilica, February 2, 2015. (www.vatican.va).

**Page 47:** We can imagine this tiny family . . . Angelus, St. Peter's Square, December 28, 2014. (www.vatican.va).

**Page 47:** Jesus is he who brings generations closer. . . . Angelus, St. Peter's Square, December 28, 2014. (www.vatican.va).

**Page 47:** The baby Jesus with his mother, Mary . . . Angelus, St. Peter's Square, December 28, 2014. (www.vatican.va).

**Page 48:** The Gospel of Matthew tells us how . . . Angelus, St. Peter's Square, December 29, 2013. (www.vatican.va).

**Page 48:** In distant lands, even when they find work . . . Angelus, St. Peter's Square, December 29, 2013. (www.vatican.va).

**Page 48:** Jesus wanted to belong to a family who experienced . . . Angelus, St. Peter's Square, December 29, 2013. (www.vatican.va).

**Page 49:** Jesus dwelt on [the] periphery . . . General Audience, December 17, 2014. (www.vatican.va).

**Page 49:** We are certainly moved by the story . . . General Audience, December 17, 2014. (www.vatican.va).

**Page 50:** What happened in those thirty years in Nazareth . . . General Audience, December 17, 2014. (www.vatican.va).

**Page 50:** We hear the same message in the apostle Paul's . . . Homily, St. Peter's Square, September 28, 2014. (www.vatican.va).

**Page 50:** St. Paul urges Timothy, who was a pastor . . . Homily, St. Peter's Square, September 28, 2014. (www.vatican.va).

**Page 50:** Today our gaze on the Holy Family . . . Angelus, St. Peter's Square, December 29, 2013. (www.vatican.va).

**Page 51:** Let us fervently call upon Mary Most Holy . . . Angelus, St. Peter's Square, December 29, 2013. (www.vatican.va).

**Page 53:** In Matthew 22:15–21 Jesus reminds us that the whole of divine law . . . Angelus, St. Peter's Square, October 26, 2014. (www.vatican.va).

**Page 53:** In effect, the visible sign a Christian can show . . . Angelus, St. Peter's Square, October 26, 2014. (www.vatican.va).

**Page 54:** In Exodus 22:22–26 we see that the requirement to be holy . . . Angelus, St. Peter's Square, October 26, 2014. (www.vatican.va).

**Page 54:** Now, in the light of this Word of Jesus, . . . Angelus, St. Peter's Square, October 26, 2014. (www.vatican.va).

**Page 54:** In the middle of the dense forest of rules and regulations . . . Angelus, St. Peter's Square, October 26, 2014. (www.vatican.va).

**Page 54:** The prophet Isaiah presents [Divine Providence] as the image of maternal . . . Angelus, St. Peter's Square, March 2, 2014. (www.vatican.va).

**Page 55:** However, thinking of the many people who live in precarious . . . Angelus, St. Peter's Square, March 2, 2014. (www.vatican.va).

**Page 55:** God's providence comes through our service to others . . . Angelus, St. Peter's Square, March 2, 2014. (www.vatican.va).

**Page 55:** A heart troubled by the desire for possessions . . . Angelus, St. Peter's Square, March 2, 2014. (www.vatican.va).

**Page 55:** The road Jesus points out can seem a little unrealistic . . . Angelus, St. Peter's Square, March 2, 2014. (www.vatican.va).

**Page 56:** The Gospel of Matthew 4:1–11 sets before us the narrative . . . Angelus, St. Peter's Square, March 9, 2014. (www.vatican.va).

**Page 56:** The tempter seeks to divert Jesus from the Father's plan . . . Angelus, St. Peter's Square, March 9, 2014. (www.vatican.va).

**Page 56:** Jesus decisively rejects all these temptations . . . Angelus, St. Peter's Square, March 9, 2014. (www.vatican.va).

**Page 56:** Let us remember this: at the moment of temptation . . . Angelus, St. Peter's Square, March 9, 2014. (www.vatican.va).

**Page 57:** The Bible tells us that the great threat to God's . . . Homily, Rizal Park, Manila, January 18, 2015. (www.vatican.va).

**Page 57:** The poor are at the center of the Gospel . . . Homily, Cathedral of the Immaculate Conception, Manila, January 16, 2015. (www.vatican.va).

**Page 58:** In Matthew's Gospel we find Jesus' invitation . . . Angelus, St. Peter's Square, July 6, 2014. (www.vatican.va).

**Page 58:** This invitation of Jesus reaches to our day . . . Angelus, St. Peter's Square, July 6, 2014. (www.vatican.va).

**Page 58:** Indifference: human indifference causes the needy . . . Angelus, St. Peter's Square, July 6, 2014. (www.vatican.va).

**Page 58:** Jesus promises to give rest to everyone, . . . Angelus, St. Peter's Square, July 6, 2014. (www.vatican.va).

**Page 59:** From this event we can understand three messages . . . Angelus, St. Peter's Square, August 3, 2014. (www.vatican.va).

**Page 59:** Jesus is like this: he suffers together with us . . . Angelus, St. Peter's Square, August 3, 2014. (www.vatican.va).

**Page 59:** The second message is *sharing* . . . Angelus, St. Peter's Square, August 3, 2014. (www.vatican.va).

**Page 60:** How many times we turn away so as not . . . Angelus, St. Peter's Square, August 3, 2014. (www.vatican.va).

**Page 60:** So many men and women of faith have faith . . . Homily, Santa Marta, February 20, 2015. (www.vatican.va).

**Page 60:** *Compassion, sharing.* And the third message . . . Angelus, St. Peter's Square, August 3, 2014. (www.vatican.va).

**Page 61:** The biblical and Christian vision of time and history . . . Homily, Vatican Basilica, December 31, 2013. (www.vatican.va).

**Page 61:** *Walking*—this verb makes us reflect on the course of history . . . Homily, Vatican Basilica, December 24, 2013. (www.vatican.va).

**Page 61:** [Jesus] has entered our history; he has shared our journey . . . Homily, Vatican Basilica, December 24, 2013. (www.vatican.va).

**Page 62:** The Gospel account of the Magi (Matt. 2:1–12) . . . Angelus, St. Peter's Square, January 6, 2015. (www.vatican.va).

**Page 62:** The star that is able to lead every person to Jesus . . . Angelus, St. Peter's Square, January 6, 2015. (www.vatican.va).

**Page 62:** When one looks to Christ, one does not err. . . . Angelus, St. Peter's Square, January 6, 2015. (www.vatican.va).

**Page 63:** The apostle tells us that with the resurrection of Jesus . . . General Audience, April 10, 2013. (www.vatican.va).

**Page 63:** Remain steadfast in the journey of faith . . . Homily, St. Peter's Square, April 28, 2013. (www.vatican.va).

**Page 64:** Always remember this: life is a journey . . . Homily, First Sunday of Advent, December 1, 2013. (www.vatican.va).

**Page 64:** At the beginning of Mass, every time . . . Angelus, St. Peter's Square, September 7, 2014. (www.vatican.va).

**Page 64:** The road to Emmaus [is] a symbol of our journey . . . *Regina Caeli*, St. Peter's Square, May 4, 2014. (www.vatican.va).

**Page 65:** We know that this increasingly artificial world . . . Homily, Basilica of Santa Sabina, March 5, 2014. (www.vatican.va).

**Page 65:** In our personal history, too, there are both bright . . . Homily, Vatican Basilica, December 24, 2013. (www.vatican.va).

**Page 66:** Only when the difficulties and suffering of others . . . Homily, Basilica of Santa Sabina, March 5, 2014. (www.vatican.va).

**Page 66:** The first element is prayer. Prayer is the strength . . . Homily, Basilica of Santa Sabina, March 5, 2014. (www.vatican.va).

**Page 66:** The second key element of the Lenten journey is fasting . . . Homily, Basilica of Santa Sabina, March 5, 2014. (www.vatican.va).

**Page 66:** The third element is almsgiving: it points to giving freely . . . Homily, Basilica of Santa Sabina, March 5, 2014. (www.vatican.va).

**Page 67:** God invites us to pray insistently not because . . . Angelus, St. Peter's Square, October 20, 2013. (www.vatican.va).

**Page 67:** We, the disciples of Jesus, are called to be people . . . Angelus, St. Peter's Square, Second Sunday of Lent, March 16, 2014. (www.vatican.va).

**Page 67:** But also let us listen to Jesus in his written Word . . . Angelus, St. Peter's Square, Second Sunday of Lent, March 16, 2014. (www.vatican.va).

**Page 68:** Read the Gospel. Read the Gospel . . . Angelus, St. Peter's Square, July 27, 2014. (www.vatican.va).

**Page 68:** In addition, attending Sunday Mass . . . Angelus, St. Peter's Square, August 31, 2014. (www.vatican.va).

**Page 69:** The older theologians used to say that the soul . . . Homily, St. Peter's Square, May 19, 2013. (www.vatican.va).

**Page 69:** Speaking to the apostles at the Last Supper . . . Homily, Vatican Basilica, June 8, 2014. (www.vatican.va).

**Page 69:** A fundamental element of Pentecost is *astonishment* . . . *Regina Caeli*, St. Peter's Square, June 8, 2014. (www.vatican.va).

**Page 70:** The Holy Spirit, who has wholly animated the life . . . Angelus, St. Peter's Square, January 11, 2015. (www.vatican.va).

**Page 70:** But who is the Holy Spirit? In the Creed . . . General Audience, May 8, 2013. (www.vatican.va).

**Page 70:** The day of Pentecost, when the disciples . . . Homily, June 8, 2014. (www.vatican.va).

**Page 71:** We turn to the Virgin Mary, who in that Pentecost . . . *Regina Caeli*, St. Peter's Square, June 8, 2014. (www.vatican.va).

**Page 71**: I would like to focus especially on the fact that *the Holy Spirit* . . . General Audience, May 8, 2013. (www.vatican.va).

**Page 71**: At this point we may ask ourselves: why can . . . General Audience, May 8, 2013. (www.vatican.va).

**Page 72**: The Holy Spirit teaches us to see with the eyes of Christ . . . General Audience, May 8, 2013. (www.vatican.va).

**Page 72**: And we, do we listen to the Holy Spirit? . . . General Audience, May 8, 2013. (www.vatican.va).

**Page 72**: But there's more: the Holy Spirit also lets us speak . . . Homily, June 8, 2014. (www.vatican.va).

**Page 72**: So how does the Holy Spirit act in our life and . . . General Audience, May 15, 2013. (www.vatican.va).

**Page 73**: Some in Jerusalem would have liked Jesus' disciples . . . *Regina Caeli*, St. Peter's Square, June 8, 2014. (www.vatican.va).

**Page 73**: In truth, the Church shows her fidelity to the Holy . . . Homily, Catholic Cathedral of the Holy Spirit, Istanbul, November 29, 2014. (www.vatican.va).

**Page 73**: *Newness* always makes us a bit fearful, because . . . Homily, St. Peter's Square, May 19, 2013. (www.vatican.va).

**Page 74**: The Holy Spirit is the soul of *mission*. . . . Homily, St. Peter's Square, May 19, 2013. (www.vatican.va).

**Page 74**: In intimacy with God and in listening to his Word . . . Homily, St. Peter's Square, May 19, 2013. (www.vatican.va).

**Page 74**: Three ideas: *Go, do not be afraid,* and *serve.* . . . Homily, Waterfront of Copacabana, Rio de Janeiro, July 28, 2013. (www.vatican.va).

**Page 75**: Fear of the Lord is the gift of the Holy Spirit . . . General Audience, June 11, 2014. (www.vatican.va).

**Page 75**: Fear of the Lord allows us to be aware that everything . . . General Audience, June 11, 2014. (www.vatican.va).

**Page 75**: Yet, we should take care, for the gift of God . . . General Audience, June 11, 2014. (www.vatican.va).

**Page 76**: I would like to add a word about another particular . . . General Audience, May 1, 2013. (www.vatican.va).

**Page 76**: I am thinking of those who live off human trafficking . . . General Audience, June 11, 2014. (www.vatican.va).

**Page 76:** Fear of the Lord, therefore, does not make of us Christians . . . General Audience, June 11, 2014. (www.vatican.va).

**Page 76:** Dear friends, Psalm 34 tells us to pray like this . . . General Audience, June 11, 2014. (www.vatican.va).

**Page 79:** It is not possible "to love Christ but without the Church . . . Homily, Vatican Basilica, January 1, 2015. (www.vatican.va).

**Page 79:** Christ is the living Temple of the Father . . . General Audience, June 26, 2013. (www.vatican.va).

**Page 80:** So what is the Church born from? . . . General Audience, May 29, 2013. (www.vatican.va).

**Page 80:** The Church's activity and mission are expressions of her motherhood . . . Homily, Vatican Basilica, January 1, 2015. (www.vatican.va).

**Page 80:** What is God's plan? It is to make of us all a single family . . . General Audience, May 29, 2013. (www.vatican.va).

**Page 80:** The Church does not rest solely beneath the shadow . . . General Audience, October 9, 2013. (www.vatican.va).

**Page 81:** What can I, a weak fragile sinner, do? . . . General Audience, October 2, 2013. (www.vatican.va).

**Page 81:** We can say that [the Church] is like family life. In the family . . . General Audience, October 9, 2013. (www.vatican.va).

**Page 82:** One's thought goes in the first place . . . General Audience, June 25, 2014. (www.vatican.va).

**Page 82:** Our witness is to make others understand what it means to be Christian . . . General Audience, October 29, 2014. (www.vatican.va).

**Page 83:** Mary is so closely united to Jesus because she received . . . Homily, Vatican Basilica, January 1, 2015. (www.vatican.va).

**Page 83:** At the message of the angel, Mary does not hide her surprise . . . Homily, St. Peter's Square, October 13, 2013. (www.vatican.va).

**Page 83:** At the Annunciation, the Messenger of God calls Mary "full of grace" . . . General Audience, October 23, 2013. (www.vatican.va).

**Page 84:** How did Mary live this faith? She lived . . . General Audience, October 23, 2013. (www.vatican.va).

**Page 84:** [W]e can also praise [God] and glorify him, like the shepherds . . . Homily, Vatican Basilica, January 1, 2015. (www.vatican.va).

**Page 84:** *Mary [is] the model of charity.* In what way is Mary a living example . . . General Audience, October 23, 2013. (www.vatican.va).

**Page 85:** *Mary [is] the model of union with Christ.* The life of . . . General Audience, October 23, 2013. (www.vatican.va).

**Page 85:** Mary says, "My soul glorifies the Lord." Today . . . Homily, Castel Gandolfo, August 15, 2013. (www.vatican.va).

**Page 85:** Mary also experienced the martyrdom of the cross . . . Homily, Castel Gandolfo, August 15, 2013. (www.vatican.va).

**Page 85:** Along our path, which is often difficult, we are not alone . . . Homily, Square in front of the Shrine of Our Lady of Bonaria, Cagliari, September 22, 2013. (www.vatican.va).

**Page 86:** Mary has always been present in the hearts of the Christian people . . . Homily, Vatican Basilica, January 1, 2014. (www.vatican.va).

**Page 86:** Our pilgrimage of faith has been inseparably linked to Mary . . . Homily, Vatican Basilica, January 1, 2014. (www.vatican.va).

**Page 86:** The Mother of the Redeemer goes before us . . . Homily, Vatican Basilica, Wednesday, January 1, 2014. (www.vatican.va).

**Page 87:** Let us not be afraid to go out and look upon our brothers . . . Homily, Square in front of the Shrine of Our Lady of Bonaria, Cagliari, September 22, 2013. (www.vatican.va).

**Page 89:** The Feast of All Saints that we are celebrating today reminds . . . Angelus, St. Peter's Square, November 1, 2013. (www.vatican.va).

**Page 89:** And on All Saints' Day and the first day that we commemorate . . . Homily, Cemetery of Verano, November 1, 2013. (www.vatican.va).

**Page 89:** Through this feast, the saints give us a message . . . Angelus, St. Peter's Square, November 1, 2013. (www.vatican.va).

**Page 90:** Saints are people who for love of God did not put conditions . . . Angelus, St. Peter's Square, November 1, 2013. (www.vatican.va).

**Page 90:** Being holy is not a privilege for the few, as if someone . . . Angelus, St. Peter's Square, November 1, 2013. (www.vatican.va).

**Page 90:** If we are rooted in the source of Love, which is God . . . General Audience, October 30, 2013. (www.vatican.va).

**Page 90:** The communion of saints goes *beyond earthly life, beyond death* . . . General Audience, October 30, 2013. (www.vatican.va).

**Page 91:** We should all ask ourselves: How do I bear witness to Christ . . . Homily, Basilica of Saint Paul Outside-the-Walls, April 14, 2013. (www.vatican.va).

**Page 91:** There are the saints of every day, the "hidden" saints . . . Homily, Basilica of Saint Paul Outside-the-Walls, April 14, 2013. (www.vatican.va).

**Page 91:** The saints are not supermen, nor were they born perfect. . . . Angelus, St. Peter's Square, November 1, 2013. (www.vatican.va).

**Page 92:** It is happening today. It seems that these . . . Homily, Cemetery of Verano, November 1, 2014. (www.vatican.va).

**Page 92:** In fact, the Kingdom of Heaven is for those who do not place . . . Angelus, St. Peter's Square, November 1, 2013. (www.vatican.va).

# About the Editor and Compiler

**James P. Campbell** has over 40 years of experience as a catechist and national speaker in Catholic religious education. He received a BA and MA degree in European History, and later an MA in theology and a Doctor of Ministry in Christian Education from Aquinas Institute of Theology.

In the 12 years previous to retirement, Jim was Staff Theologian at Loyola Press and is the co-author of *Finding God: Our Response to God's Gifts*, Grades 1–8. Jim has also written *Stories of the Old Testament: A Catholic's Guide*, and *Mary and the Saints: Companions on the Journey*.

# Learn More About Pope Francis and His Message of Mercy

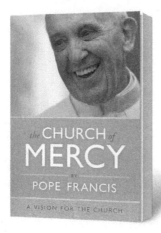

## The Church of Mercy
*A Vision for the Church*

Collected from Pope Francis's speeches, homilies, and papers presented during the first year of his papacy, *The Church of Mercy* is the first Vatican-authorized book detailing his vision for the Catholic Church. This book's deep wisdom reminds us that the Church must move beyond its own walls and joyfully bring God's mercy wherever suffering, division, or injustice exists.

Hardcover | 4168-0 | $22.95
Paperback | 4170-3 | $16.95
Discussion Guide 10-Pack | 4204-5 | $9.95

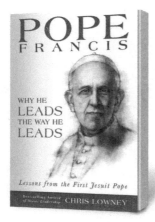

## Pope Francis: Why He Leads the Way He Leads
*Lessons from the First Jesuit Pope*

Best-selling author and former Jesuit seminarian Chris Lowney offers an in-depth look at how Pope Francis's Jesuit training has directly impacted his various leadership roles and what it suggests about how he might lead in the future. Readers will gain essential lessons to help them with their own leadership challenges.

Hardcover | 4008-9 | $22.95
Paperback | 4091-1 | $16.95

# Learn More About Pope Francis and His Message of Mercy

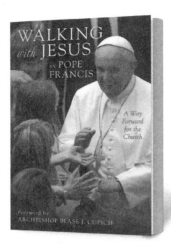

## Walking with Jesus
### *A Way Forward for the Church*

In *Walking with Jesus: A Way Forward for the Church*, Pope Francis urges us to make Jesus central in our individual lives and in the collective life of the Church. With a foreword by Archbishop of Chicago Blase J. Cupich, Vatican-authorized *Walking with Jesus* offers the Church a much-needed way forward as it fearlessly follows Christ toward the future.

Hardcover | 4248-9 | $22.95
Paperback | 4254-0 | $16.95

## Pope Francis
### *Life and Revolution*

Written by Vatican correspondent Elisabetta Piqué, who has known the Pope personally since 2001, *Pope Francis: Life and Revolution* offers unique insights into how the Pope thinks and feels; his work for the poor; and his vision for the Church. Piqué reveals the personal side of Pope Francis and the profoundly spiritual influence of his Jesuit formation on the man who now leads the Catholic Church.

Hardcover | 4213-7 | $22.95
Paperback | 4217-5 | $16.95

**TO ORDER:** Call 800.621.1008, visit www.loyolapress.com/store, or visit your local bookseller.

# From the Irish Jesuits

## Sacred Space
### *The Prayer Book 2016*

The secret to Sacred Space's popularity is its simplicity. At its core is a simple daily prayer based on scripture, and *Sacred Space: The Prayer Book* offers reflections for every day of the liturgical year.

Each day of *Sacred Space: The Prayer Book* includes Scripture readings and points of reflection, as well as a weekly topic enhanced by six steps of prayer and reflection: The Presence of God, Freedom, Consciousness, The Word, Conversation, and Conclusion. It is the ideal gift for your parish, campus ministry program, small group, friend, family member, or yourself.

Paperback | 4367-7 | $15.95

## Sacred Space for Advent and the Christmas Season 2015–2016

Paperback | 4368-4 | $1.25

## Sacred Space for Lent 2016

Paperback | 4370-7 | $1.75

*Sacred Space* is updated each fall for the new liturgical calendar.

# A Young Woman Lives Out the Call for Mercy

## Mercy in the City
How to Feed the Hungry, Give Drink to the Thirsty,
Visit the Imprisoned, and Keep Your Day Job

Kerry Weber

Pb • 3892-5 • $13.95

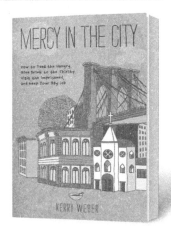

*Mercy in the City* is Kerry Weber's story of
exploring the challenges and rewards that
accompany a lay Catholic trying to practice
the Seven Corporal Works of Mercy in
New York City.

---

# An Invitation to Encounter Christ in a Whole New Way

## Under the Influence of Jesus
The Transforming Experience
of Encountering Christ

Joe Paprocki

Pb • 4050-8 • $15.95

In *Under the Influence of Jesus,* best-selling
author Joe Paprocki explores the particular
characteristics of a changed heart and life that
result from accepting Jesus' message. *Under the
Influence of Jesus* is ultimately an invitation to
encounter Christ in a whole new way, to thrive
under his lordship, and to use our own transformed hearts and lives to
help bring others into a life-changing relationship with Jesus.

# Continue the Conversation
# at LoyolaPress.com

If you enjoyed this book, then connect with Loyola Press to continue the conversation, engage with other readers, and find out about new and upcoming books from your favorite spiritual writers.

Visit us at **www.LoyolaPress.com** to create an account and register for our newsletters. Or scan the code below with your smartphone.

Connect with us through:

 **Facebook**
facebook.com
/loyolapress

 **Twitter**
twitter.com
/loyolapress

 **YouTube**
youtube.com
/loyolapress

# Ignatian Spirituality
## www.ignatianspirituality.com

## Visit us online to

- Join our E-Magis newsletter
- Pray the Daily Examen
- Make an online retreat with the *Ignatian Prayer Adventure*
- Participate in the conversation with the dotMagis blog and at **facebook.com/ignatianspirituality**